Chris Kulikowski 881
Bb Kulikowski 8411

OPEN SECRETS

A Poor Person's Life in Higher Education

Betty Brown-Chappell, PhD, LMSW

This work is set in Cambria typeface. Formatting follows the guidelines set forth in the *Publication Manual of the American Psychological Association, 6th Edition,* with some layout modifications required by the publisher.

An abbreviated electronic (pdf) version is available online at DigitalCommons@EMU (http://commons.emich.edu/).

Dedication

Dr. Pastora San Juan Cafferty

Dr. Dolores "Dodie" Norton

Table of Contents

Handwritten margin notes: *5 Points per Paper*; *2-3 Paragraphs*

Acknowledgements vii

Preface ix

Chapter 1 – Introduction... 1

Chapter 2 – Strawberry Lessons 13

Chapter 3 – The Nuts and Bolts of Gettin' Over: Childhood

to Grad School 21

Chapter 4 – Family Matters: Walking the Path, Family, and

the Achievement Gap.. 45

Photo Album 75

Chapter 5 – Isms: Classism, Racism, and Sexism 85

Chapter 6 – The Nuts and Bolts of Gettin' Over: The

Doctoral Program 117

Chapter 7 – Tenure the Game... 141

Chapter 8 – Lessons from the Second Generation....... 157

Chapter 9 – Blueberry Blessings: Conclusion 173

Appendix 177

Acknowledgements

Autoethnography involves the reflections of an individual; as author of this book, I am solely responsible for the content. However, I am indebted to many family members who have reviewed the manuscript: Michael, Jahi, and Aisha Chappell were joined in this endeavor by my siblings Frances Ray, Gail Patterson, and Ben Brown, as well as my cousin Linda Dixon and brother-in-law Aaron E. Ray. Friends and colleagues have assisted me with the interminable drafts: Ann Rosegrant Alvarez, Pastora San Juan Cafferty, Melvin Peters, Pavritha Narayanan, Desiree Hellegers, Pamela Gesund, Dara Walker, and Annarosa Mendoza-King. Professor Julia Nims of the Halle Library Digital Commons has demonstrated extraordinary patience and support during the publishing process. I am grateful for the comments of both McNair Scholars at Eastern Michigan University and social policy students enrolled at Eastern Michigan University during 2010. David Erik Nelson, my writing coach, provided me with much-needed encouragement and technical writing guidance, and both Sarah Primeau and Lisa Walters provided copyediting. I owe particular thanks to Dr. Sarah Huyvaert who pointed out many years ago that failure to publish this book meant that I believed in the negative judgments of others in society. She urged me repeatedly to tell this story and to realize its value.

A couple of years ago, I sent an early draft of this book to Dr. San Juan Cafferty, my dissertation chairperson. In brief her comments were quite favorable, although she said that she believed that I gave her "entirely too much credit" as I recounted the events that led to the award of my doctorate degree. Unfortunately, she left this world on April 16, 2013. As I reflect on the enormous void she left behind, I think, "Pastora, this is one time you are wrong. You did not receive too much credit for what you contributed to my life."

Preface

I have been blessed. Not because I was born into the good life of wealth and luxury. Quite the contrary: I was blessed by birth into the hardship of poverty, the hatred of racism, and the prerogatives of sexism. I was a child of African-American parents whose passionate love for each other proved to be the spark that created a nurturing family life for eight children, each of whom would finish college and beyond. Poverty meant that my parents' children achieved often without the benefit of routine medical or dental care, many times while wearing rummage-sale or hand-me-down clothes. Franklin and Lucille Brown struggled to provide us with books and supplies during the first weeks of class. When they tried and failed to protect me from the rocks hurled at me by other kids or from the racial slur *nigger* yelled at school by White classmates, they taught me how to fight for myself and later to protect my siblings. Although women generally took a subservient role to men when I grew up in the 1950s and '60s, my parents stressed higher education, especially for their five daughters, as a way to ensure the "good life."

During the six-plus decades of my life I have far exceeded every childhood dream I ever had. Many of my experiences, and the accomplishments that I list on my resume, sound unrealistic or even boastful when taken together or mentioned in casual conversation. Since I left rural southwestern Michigan, where I was educated in a one-room school house until the age of twelve, I have had the good fortune to attend two presidential inaugural balls, to meet then-U. S. Senator Barack Obama, and to know our state's first woman governor and many in our state's congressional delegation. I had these opportunities because, once I finished graduate education at the University of Michigan, I made a pledge to myself that I would try to be part of the solution rather than part of the problem, to advocate with and for other poor and oppressed people, especially those least able to help themselves such as children, the elderly, and the disabled. My pledge to become an advocate helped me to overcome the usual hesitance people have to speak out to power whether on the job, in the community, or within my profession. This is how I became involved with politics and how I ultimately met many policymakers.

My parents valued education, creativity, and thrift. They believed President John F. Kennedy when he said that every child who had the ability to do so could attend college. Hence, they were very proud of my college admission and wished me well when I left home to attend the University of Michigan. Rather than financial support—my parents still had to care for seven minor children—they gave me an almost fanatical belief in myself despite the fact that I arrived for college with only $400 in cash and no job or scholarships. I made my way because thankfully my trials, within the larger society, were lessened by the untold numbers of lives that were risked and lost in the African-American struggle for educational and employment opportunity.[1] I learned about the financial aid programs for African Americans and others from low-income families that resulted from this struggle when I met Nu Chapter members of Delta Sigma Theta Sorority. Eventually, I learned how to couple these program funds with part-time jobs and frugal spending habits. My belief in myself was fortified at the University of Michigan because I learned to excel and to creatively problem-solve from some of the best minds in the country.

---

[1]The struggle for racial equality in all aspects of life for Blacks has been ably discussed in a trilogy of books by Taylor Branch who won a Pulitzer Prize for one of his works; these books span the years 1954-68. Similarly, detailed discussions of Black life in the urban north and south are provided respectively by St. Clair Drake and Horace Cayton (1945) in *The Black Metropolis* and Isabel Wilkerson (2010) in *The Warmth of Other Suns.* These are but a few of the very competent works on the struggle that yielded the policies that helped me and many others.

My academic experience at University of Michigan further reinforced my inborn sense that I could overcome obstacles, such as the oppression of poverty, racism, and sexism. Given my self-confidence, my training, and my pledge to advocate for others, I am often a contentious employee, volunteer, advocate, and citizen. Practically, what this means is that I have testified before Congress on welfare reform; attended a United Nations conference hosted by the Secretary-General; successfully pushed for merit scholarship money for poor and underrepresented students at University of Chicago and Eastern Michigan University; organized a picket of the civil rights office where I worked; studied how Black mayors lead and taught those lessons to social workers and poor communities; lectured on social change in Eastern Europe; and discussed my work on radio, television, and in many print media such as the *New York Times* and *Ebony Magazine*. These efforts have not always been well-received by my employers, friends, family, and professional associates, to the extent that I was once fired (and rehired within 24 hours) because of a stand that I took.

I believe that it is a travesty for anyone who has the talent and desire to achieve to be held back because they do not know where the next stepping stones are or because they are afraid of social backlash. This book is an extension of my pledge to advocate for others who are poor and underrepresented and who believe that they can learn by example. In learning from others I have gained a life rich in excitement and achievement, and I am so grateful to all those who took the extra time, often at great personal cost, to care for me and help me on my journey. Although I am proud of the hard-won lessons and accomplishments in my life, they would not be possible without the love, dedication, and support of my teachers, mentors, and friends. I especially treasure my life partner and dear husband, Michael, and our children, Jahi and Aisha Chappell. I truly stand on the shoulders of these giants.

Chapter 1 — Introduction

I am an angry Black woman. This is a secret and has been so most of my life. I am angry because the social justice—righting of historic and contemporary racist and sexist wrongs—that I expected for myself and my people has eluded America for the sixty-plus years that I have been on earth, in addition to the centuries that passed before. Although I learned to live with what Close (1993) calls the "Rage of a privileged class," like many people of color, women, and poor people, I have been the target of exclusion and derision. I have been the target of social exclusion and slights, but more importantly, of economic losses caused by employment discrimination used by and on behalf of the dominant or ruling group (upper class, White, and, most of the time, male) to keep their place at the top of the ladder; I have been stoned as I heard the taunts of *nigger* in grammar school; and I have experienced the violence of rape.

This book seeks to open the secrets of my experience with oppression as a Black woman who moved successfully through a series of educational institutions as both student and professor. I attempt to reveal the secrets/realizations about my life; from them I derive lessons for others who may share my sense of distance from the mainstream, yet who seek to survive and thrive there.

Most of what I have to say is not truly a secret, especially if one knows what to look for, so what may seem to be a secret is in fact already in public view.

Survival in the mainstream has a price. Many years ago my doctoral advisor at the University of Chicago, Dolores "Dodie" Norton, helped me to understand that even the calmest, most placid African American is likely to experience a sense of disaffection from the mainstream. Not only do Blacks who "make it" often have extensive knowledge of past wrongs (perhaps gained as part of their education and home teaching), but also their skin color (and I add female gender) marks them forever to the larger culture as an outcast to be denigrated, dismissed, and destroyed. Some daily examples may give the reader a sense of how flimsy our career and academic achievements might seem to us. For example, frequently when I am the next person in a line, the sales associate walks to the White person behind me to ask if he or she needs assistance. Another of my "favorite" slights is when those who visit my office approach me and request to speak to the person in charge; for all the decades of my career I have had to patiently explain that I am the person they seek. One of the most celebrated cases of misplaced racial and class identity involved the 2009 mistaken identity of Harvard Professor Henry Louis Gates when he was stopped as he entered his own home because the police officer suspected him of breaking and entering. Gates's experience is not unlike an instance when a police officer asked me (when I was an Assistant Dean at the University of Chicago) to move along and quit loitering in front of the President's annual welcome party.

To cope with this devaluation by the dominant culture Dubois (1903) argued, similar to Norton et al. (1978), that Blacks operate with a "twoness" of behavior where one uses the knowledge, manners, dress, and verbal cadences of the dominant culture to navigate in professional situations (and if one is good at it, to gain a measure of success) while one alternatively speaks, acts, and dresses appropriate to the Black world where one most likely passes all non-professional time. Those who are good at "twoness" have what Norton et al. (1978) identifies as a dual perspective.

The ability to behave within both the dominant American and numeric minority culture has also been identified by other authors writing decades apart. First, Stonequist (1930) detailed the dilemma of the "marginal man" when he discussed Jewish citizens' resolution of their religious "twoness." More recently, Diversi and Moreira (2009) provide a jarring ethnographic illustration of their experiences as immigrants who study and work in America's higher education institutions:

> In Brazil, where we were born, we are called *gringos* by the folks we work with. In the U.S.A., where we live, the establishment calls us aliens. We call ourselves *betweeners*: (un)conscious bodies experiencing life in and between two cultures. (p. 19)

This last discussion is both gut-wrenching and angry as the authors provide first-person accounts and theoretical comments on the nature and improbability of their journey as witnesses to life and death in Brazil where they work with street children. Simultaneously, the two men discuss their doctoral education against the backdrop of America's sometimes dehumanizing and artificial expectations for theories and research rigor.

This brings me full circle to my own anger about the seemingly intractable problem of racial and social injustice. The specific targets of my anger are colleges and universities that fail to graduate students who are more often than not poor, minority, and first-generation (meaning the first in their family to graduate with a college degree). Such institutions know how to graduate "the upper crust" because it is this type of student that the institutions are best suited to serve. I argue here, similar to Roderick (2011), that low-graduation rates are a tragedy, an injustice perpetrated upon the students, their families, and the taxpayers or donors who financially underwrite such schools. Further, when students experience years in college and do not obtain a degree, yet still have the burden of tens of thousands of dollars of loans plus interest charges, then I maintain that the tragedy amounts to financial fraud.

To me this fraud, this tragedy, is very close to home. According to a report issued by the Business Leaders for Michigan (2013), first-year students enrolled at my university have approximately a 40% possibility of graduation after six years of enrollment.

Calling attention to such injustice (and waste of government resources), President Obama noted in his 2013 State of the Union speech that the federal government will soon take steps to address the issue. He said, "I ask Congress to change the Higher Education Act, so that affordability and value are included in determining which colleges receive . . . federal aid" (Obama, 2013, p. 3, para. 4). He also indicated that the federal government would release a "College Scorecard" so students and parents can make informed decisions about this important financial investment.

Too often the problem of failure to graduate involves students with the talent and desire to achieve who just cannot locate the stepping stones to graduation, and who may lack the moral support from family and friends to achieve this goal. Over 40 years ago when I graduated from undergraduate school at the University of Michigan, I pledged to myself that I would advocate for other poor and underrepresented people. My path through higher education involved finding out about some "open secrets" of higher education from books, mentors, role models, friends, and—as my mother would call it—"the school of hard knocks." That is, I learned from my many mistakes as I pursued and earned bachelor, master, and doctoral degrees. Thus, the first aim of this book is to share what I have learned as I walked this path with others who may also be from those underrepresented in the legions of graduates from America's institutions of higher education. According to federal anti-poverty programs in higher education, those left behind or who are in danger of being left behind include African American, Asian and Pacific Islanders, Native American, or Latino Americans. Such students may also be from low-income families who have no history of college graduation.

Second, I want to provide professional educators or counselors with some insights to help them to better serve such students. This book can serve as a focal point of social work, human services, educational counseling, or youth discussions as it offers some scenarios for students to contemplate future educational predicaments in what was for me, and might be for them, a strange new world of obstacles and opportunities presented by institutions of higher education. Finally, this book may not only be instructive to low-income students and educational professionals, but it may also be read more broadly by parents and guardians who want to help their loved ones make a reality out of their dream of college graduation.

The following discussion establishes this book within its academic context and may be skipped by those outside of higher education.

This work uses auto-ethnographic methods of reflection on the transitions of life within a cultural context (Spry, 2011; Diversi & Moreira, 2009; Ellis, 2003). This technique means that I use events from my life as a (formerly) poor African-American female to illustrate educational and class dilemmas during the period of 1946 to the present. I act within the cultural context (political, economic, and social) of an America where institutions and individuals often devalued or prejudged me because of my brown skin, poverty at birth, and female gender. Thus, I both act and am being acted upon within a cultural context that is ever-changing. There is a similar method of reflection that I have used in my class on gerontology and practice with aging people that is called "life course review": an examination of one's biological characteristics as they are acted upon by the social, political, and economic forces plus major societal events such as riots, wars, and natural disasters.

One example of cultural change within the political arena serves to illustrate the degree of change within my lifetime. When I was born in 1946, the president of the United States was Harry Truman, a White man from Missouri, a state with a history of ambivalence towards Blacks that pre-dated the Civil War. In contrast, the current president, Barack Obama, was born in Hawai'i, a racially diverse state, and is the child of an African father and a Caucasian American woman (McCullough, 1992; Obama, 1995). President Obama is recognized as the first African-American or Black president in the history of our country. I submit that the policies of both leaders impacted my life to some degree.

While not identified as autoethnography, there are also a number of best-selling books based on the authors' experiences that attempt to illustrate the dilemmas of poverty or poverty and race. Ehrenreich's (2002) *Nickel and Dimed*, Gardner's (2006) *The Pursuit of Happyness*, and Walls's (2005) *The Glass Castle* are other first-person accounts of poverty which are often assigned in introductory policy classes to reinforce the need for policy solutions. *Nickel*, most similar to investigative reporting, was written to test how practical the newly-passed welfare reform laws were during the Clinton administration, while *Pursuit* and *Castle* are memoirs that were written for general audiences. While *Nickel* used policy responses to poverty as a case study it is now quite dated, the other two books were not intended for the specific purpose of teaching or guiding first-generation college graduates and their families.

Chapters from Polite's (1999) *African American Males in School and Society* detail the travails of an orphaned inner-city youth who ultimately achieved worldwide success and can also be used to teach such content. Similarly useful is Carl S. McNair's

(2006) *In the Spirit of Ronald E. McNair, Astronaut, an American Hero,* which offers a unified, although second-person, account of the path to the doctorate degree. Both works are excellent qualitative accounts of the challenges and triumphs on the paths to the doctoral degree, but Polite focuses narrowly on preparing urban educators, and McNair's book is a biography of his brother's life. Neither book explicitly states lessons about how to obtain higher degrees.

Since first-person accounts on this topic are so rare, Peters's *Getting What You Came For* (1997) is frequently assigned to the 850,000 students annually enrolled in educational anti-poverty programs. This book describes the formal and informal norms which pertain to application, matriculation, graduation, and employment in the undergraduate and graduate academic arena. However, Peters devotes only some thirty pages of his entire discussion to issues of sexual and racial diversity and provides little guidance for poor, first-generation, or underrepresented minority students. Furthermore, this work now needs to be updated or replaced, as its point of reference is more than a dozen years old. I have found that Lieberman's (2010) *Women in Social Work Who Have Changed the World* speaks more directly to women's issues than does Peters, but it excludes men who may be first-generation and low-income.

Green and Scott's (2003) *Journey to the Ph. D.* is most similar to the one proposed because it provides the aspiring doctoral student with an edited anthology discussing three main themes: entrance into the academy, adapting to the academy, and surviving the academy. The purpose of *Journey* is similar to mine: It seeks to assist those who plan to obtain a doctoral degree by providing examples of problems and solutions involved in the process. However, there are three primary differences between this book and that of Green and Scott. First, the authors have produced an edited volume that draws on the experiences of a multitude of individuals. Second, the relative youth of the contributors means generally that they have yet to attain reappointment, tenure, and promotion. They are writing more as students and less as permanent members of the academy. The third difference is that Green and Scott's work is not written for consumption by an interested but non-degreed parent or even a first-generation student who might be intimidated by the more academic tone of their work.

Thus, this book intends to fill a gap in *subject, time,* and *place* with a unified discussion of one individual's qualitative experiences of poverty, sexism, and racism, while it also advances the reader's understanding of the importance of cultural context for low-income, first-generation, underrepresented students as they matriculate through life *and* institutions of higher education. In *Open Secrets*, I seek to provide a framework for success to students in anti-poverty programs such as one that I formerly administered.

Following this "Introduction," which explains the goals and methods of the book, in Chapter 2, "Strawberry Lessons," I illustrate how a positive childhood label used by my parents—in this instance, *smart*—motivated me to achieve. I offer for the reader's consideration several lessons that I gained from this experience.

"The Nuts and Bolts of Gettin' Over: Childhood to Grad School," Chapter 3, frames my life in terms of the generations who went before me: sharecroppers, laborers, maids, and housewives. These kinfolks' lives provided me with the foundation necessary to graduate from the University of Michigan with bachelor and master degrees, plus from the University of Chicago with a doctoral degree. I then detail the obstacles presented by my status as a first-generation college and graduate school student and discuss some of the solutions that I discovered. I describe and define admission to college and the master's program, financial aid, and competition among doctoral students.

Chapter 4, "Family Matters: Walking the Path and the Achievement Gap," is my answer to the question often posed by my program participants and students: Will I lose touch with my family if I go on for a doctoral degree? I present scenarios that involve my relationships with my husband, parents, children, friends, and extended family from undergraduate through doctoral study. Photographs of my life follow this chapter.

Chapter 5, "Isms: Classism, Racism, and Sexism" identifies "isms" challenges that I faced during childhood, phases of my early career, and while I obtained a higher education. As a low-income person I learned "how to spin straw into gold"; how to deal with on-the-job conflict; and how to fight back when others tried to victimize me.

In Chapter 6, "Nuts and Bolts of Gettin' Over: The Doctoral Program" I discuss my transition from a professional social worker who was responsible to administer agencies to a doctoral student.

Chapter 7, "Tenure the Game" demystifies the various steps one takes to obtain permanent employment in an academic setting (tenure); I explain the process as a series of "game maneuvers" played out by the university as employer and the untenured faculty member as employee.

Chapter 8, "Lessons from the Second Generation" is intended primarily for parents and educators as they seek to provide guidance and support to high school and college students who aspire to graduate from a college or university. I use the examples of my two very different but successful children to suggest how one can support, challenge, and motivate students from grade school through the doctoral degree. From these experiences I draw lessons and suggest how to maintain positive relationships with one's adult children.

Chapter 9, "Blueberry Blessings: Conclusion" is a summary of what I have learned on my educational journey thus far. All of the chapters have summary lessons plus questions for the reader to discuss or reflect upon. Following the book is an appendix with lessons learned as parents from both me and my husband, Michael.

References

Business Leaders for Michigan. (2013). Scorecard, Eastern Michigan University. In *Michigan performance tracker for public universities*. Retrieved from http://www.blmperformancetracker.com

Close, E. (1993). *The rage of a privileged class.* New York, NY: Harper Collins Publishers.

Diversi, M., & Moreira, C. (2009). *Betweener talk: Decolonizing knowledge production, pedagogy, & praxis.* Walnut Creek, CA: Left Coast Press.

Dubois, W. E. B. (1903). *The souls of Black folk.* Chicago, IL: McClurg and Company.

Ehrenreich, B. (2002). *Nickel and dimed: Not getting by in America.* New York, NY: Henry Holt.

Ellis, C. (2003). *The ethnographic I – A methodological novel about autoethnography.* Walnut Creek, CA: AltaMira Press.

Gardner, C. (2006). *Pursuit of happyness.* New York, NY: HarperCollins.

Green, A. L., & Scott, L. V. (2003). *Journey to the Ph. D.* Sterling, VA: Stylus Publishing.

Lieberman, A. (2010). *Women in social work who have changed the world .* Chicago, IL: Lyceum.

McCullough, D. (1992). *Truman.* New York, NY: Simon and Schuster.

McNair, C. S. (2006). *In the spirit of Ronald E. McNair, astronaut, an American hero.* Atlanta, GA: Publishing Associates, Inc.

Norton, D. et al. (1978). *Inclusion of ethnic minority content in social work curriculum.* New York, NY: Council on Social Work Education.

Obama, B. (1995). *Dreams from my father.* New York, NY: Three Rivers Press.

Obama, B. H. (2013, February 12). Full text: President Obama's 2013 State of the Union Address. *Forbes.* Retrieved from http://www.forbes.com/sites/beltway/2013/02 /12full-text-president-obama's-2013-state-of-the-union-address

Peters, R. L. (1997). *Getting what you came for.* New York, NY: Noonday Press.

Polite, V. C. (1999). A cup that runneth over. In V. Polite & J. E. Davis (Eds.), *African American males in school and society* (pp. 184-196). New York, NY: New York Teachers College Press.

Roderick, M. (2011). Pot holes on the way to college: High schools' effects in shaping urban students' participation in college application, four-year college enrollment, and college match. *Sociology of Education, 84*(3), 178-211.

Spry, T. (2011). *Body, paper, stage – writing and performing autoethnography.* Walnut Creek, CA: Left Coast Press, Inc.

Stonequist, E.V. (1930). The marginal man. Ph.D. diss. The University of Chicago.

Walls, J. (2005). *The glass castle.* New York, NY: Simon and Schuster.

Chapter 2 — Strawberry Lessons

"We can't pick these strawberries, Betty," said my mother with a tremor of fear in her voice. "There are snakes in these bushes; I saw one the other day—might have been a rattler!" The type of rattlesnake found in Michigan is called a Masasagua, and it is as poisonous as many of its counterparts. My mother had killed several of these snakes with the sharp blade of the garden hoe in the recent past. Then as a sign to other invaders she hung their bodies on the picket fence in front of our house, perhaps in hopes that their "brethren" would take heed. I guessed Mom had a point.

Yet, at six or seven years old I knew all the answers. And I also knew that if I picked a case of berries—sixteen quarts—then I would have enough money to buy a plastic wading pool. It was very hot for early summer, projected to be in the 90s by midday. This is why I *really* wanted that wading pool.

So I said, "Mom, let's take some big sticks and hit the berry bushes in front of us 'cause you always said that the snakes are more afraid of us than we are of them. And, Mom, why don't we put our winter boots on? That way the snakes can't bite our feet as we walk along with the sticks."

Dressed incongruously in blue jeans and a starched white shirt for the sweaty manual labor before us, Mom turned her beautiful mocha-brown profile to survey the acre plot of strawberries that would bring our family the money for "extras" like school books and shoes, replacement tires for the balding ones, and, I hoped, even a night at the A & W root beer stand. Mom considered this advice. "Well, your dad did say that the berries have to be picked today because they'll spoil otherwise. I would rather wait for him to get home from work, but we might lose the crop by then." Mom paused to glance over the ankle-height rows of bushy plants that grew so well that they appeared to be hedges. Our cultivated strawberry bushes were the envy of other farmers because my dad had taken great care to get just the "right" variety from a friend. Now the plants sat in all their deep dark green glory with the large red juicy berries waiting to escape the unremitting sunshine.

Stock-still in my worn bib overalls that we all called "floods" because I had outgrown the length and the pant legs were now so short that they would not get wet in the high water of a flood, I held my breath waiting for her answer. Mom seemed to gather all her strength and resolve (she was rightfully frightened by poisonous snakes) and said, "Okay. Let's put our boots on. Then let's use the sticks just like you said and see what happens."

At first we gingerly poked the sticks ahead of us while stomping firmly in the straw between the rows of bushes. Every once in a while during the two hours it took us to pick a few cases, I would sample a large shiny berry. "Betty, stop eating all the profits." Reluctantly, I obeyed Mom. More than fifty years later, it still seems that those berries, our profits, were something special: plump, dark red, juicy, and more the size of a small egg but with a much sweeter taste than any I have had since.

Although we did not run into any snakes, the tale of my solution to our dangerous dilemma became legend. Mom told Dad about my suggestion as soon as he came home from his factory job in town. He said, "Well, you are one smart little girl, and tomorrow I'm going to take you to town, and you can buy the pool as soon as we finish selling the berries." I was as proud of the compliment from my dad as I was about the money I had earned.

My dad, a muscular Black man of six foot tall, had a demeanor often as hard as the work he did. He was employed at Bohn Aluminum and Brass, which was a light manufacturing plant in South Haven, Michigan, located about 10 miles away from our farm. I hated to iron Dad's shirts and blue jeans because even after washing they often still smelled sweaty, and they had many small holes in them from the molten aluminum that he poured into molds to make automobile pistons. Dad wore gloves with tape to protect his hands from the molten metal, but often it did not do any good. Dad's hands, legs, and arms had many small burns acquired over the years spent at this job. He seemed to enjoy working the truck farm, a small farm that yields enough crops to take to market in a truck, and tending the animals that fed us and earned a little extra cash on the side. Maybe he enjoyed it because he was his own boss and because he saw himself as more successful at the combination of farming and paid labor than many of his neighboring contemporaries.

At sunrise the next day, Dad took me and my sisters to town to sell the strawberries. I could hardly contain myself in anticipation of my first-ever purchase. Unfortunately, we had to wait in what for me was an agonizingly long line to sell the berries. Looking at the semi-trailer trucks lined up to receive the berries, I asked, "Who will ever eat all these?" My dad replied, "The people in the city – Chicago." This puzzled me. I had been to Chicago and I saw a lot of people, but I could not match the number of people I had seen with the long line of huge trucks that would deliver the crops from our local farms to stores where the city people would buy them. I did not yet know the concept of a million, yet alone that more than a million people lived within hours of our home.

At long last my dad hoisted the strawberry cases up to the waiting refrigerator trucks. He was paid, and in turn I had the $7 for my pool in my grubby little hands. As promised, Dad took me to the hardware store to buy my wading pool. I chattered away at my two younger sisters about how I would enjoy the cold water after sitting in the hot car. Once we got home, Dad inflated my wading pool with a bicycle pump, and water was added from the outdoors hose. At last, I happily splashed about in the pool, impervious to the noontime sun. Then out of the corner of my eye I spied Gail and Frances as they dipped their dirty grass-covered little feet into my pool. Well, that is where I drew the line.

I pulled myself out of my cool spot and yelled, "You didn't work for this. Get out." Frances, about three years old, poked her little lip out and stood her ground, but Gail, ever the meek and sweet little lady, obeyed me.

Both my parents came running. "You have to share with your little sisters," Mom explained.

"But Mom, why? They didn't work like I did to earn this pool."

Dad said, "Well, that may be true, but you also did not pay for the gas to take those berries to market or repay me for all the work I put into growing them. Listen, what if you take the first dip and cool off? Then you can *invite* Gail and Frances in after a little while."

I whined, "Well, that's not fair, they didn't do any work."

Dad responded, "That's true, but they are too little to do a good job like you did. I know that you want to share with your little sisters because we are a family, and that's what families do."

Reluctantly I agreed, since I figured that I wasn't going to win this argument what with Dad being the youngest boy of seven; he had a lot of sympathy for those farther down in the birth order. Of course, I paraded myself to the pool and lounged for as long as possible before "inviting my sisters" into *my* wading pool. "You have to wash your dirty feet before you can get in *my* pool," I said in a huff to remind them of *my* terms and conditions. Soon we were all wading and splashing about in our underwear as we could not afford swimsuits, and it almost felt as wonderful as it had without my unwanted "guests."

I believed I was smart (as Mom and Dad later restated to relatives and friends) and that I had solved an important problem for our family: how to harvest without danger so that we could all make money. I was also secretly pleased at my ability to negotiate some private time in my pool. There is a word, "efficacy," in community organizing literature, which generally means that a community may learn a lesson from trial and error that will enable future successes, and that a success on a small scale is likely to yield larger ones. Solving this "Strawberry Problem" provided me with my first sense of efficacy: I came to believe that being smart meant finding solutions through creative thinking, working hard, and negotiating with authorities (my parents) for concessions (keeping my sisters' dirty feet out of my new wading pool at least for a while).

I still like strawberries, but they have never tasted as good as those I ate when I earned my first seven dollars to buy that little blue and white plastic wading pool.

To me the strawberry lesson is that people can solve difficult—even dangerous—problems if they think about problems creatively, are willing to take a risk, and work very hard, harder than you might originally envision. When my parents labeled me as smart early in life, this motivated many of my future achievements such as being an honor student throughout most of my elementary and high school years, graduating from the University of Michigan with a bachelor's and master's and from the University of Chicago with a doctorate. This strawberry lesson gave me the efficacy to work for the positive regard that I believe I deserved.

Once I heard a motivational speech at the beginning of a summer college prep program that my son attended at the University of Michigan's College of Engineering. The speaker, whose name I no longer remember, emphasized the importance of understanding "not just who you are but *whose* you are." That is, one should never be ego-driven but rather realize that the path through life is always taken within the context of a larger community and family culture regardless of whether the members of this reference group are present in the physical sense. Putting this more like an anthropologist who studies culture: You are always a member of a tribe. Your successes and failures reflect on others even beyond your nuclear family, and your well-being is inextricably tied to theirs.

Lessons

In this chapter I explain some of the lessons I learned during my early childhood development:

Lesson 1: If you negotiate with those who have power then you can gain a concession and make your dream (or most of it) come true.

Lesson 2: A child's self-image can be enhanced by parents who identify those actions and thought processes that help them create solutions. If you identify them as "smart," then they will likely take on this self-image and try to live up to this label.

Lesson 3: Individuals can survive and thrive within a unit of family, friends, or colleagues through cooperation rather than competition, which is the predominant ethos of American society.

Study Questions

Identify childhood lessons that you learned. How would you apply them to your pursuit of an educational goal? In your opinion, what happens to a child who does not learn the lessons of efficacy, and is it possible to learn such lessons later in life?

Chapter 3 — The Nuts and Bolts of Gettin' Over: Childhood to Grad School

Listen, little girl
I didn't go too far in school so . . .
You got to go out and change your chances,
Get an education.

Don't depend on no man for your money!
Use your brain – then you won't have to sweat and hurt
like I did.

My father, Benjamin Franklin Brown, told me this when I was a teen.

My grandfather, a sharecropper, moved to rural Michigan on a long run from the law in Kentucky, where family lore has it that he killed someone in the early 1900s. [2] Grandfather's wife and

---

[2] Lending credibility to the family lore about Grandfather Brown's fugitive status is the fact that Sunset Memorial Lawns Cemetery in Northbrook, IL, has a gravestone in the family plot for Garfield Brown, but their office records do not match this; those records list Thomas

children followed him by rail in such haste that the oldest, a teenage boy, was accidentally left behind and neighbors had to help him to board a separate train; the youngest son was my dad, Benjamin. Meanwhile, my mom, Clara Lucille, ultimately became a foster child to a Black doctor and his wife in Waco, Texas, after the death of both her parents. Although Mom graduated from high school and qualified for admission to college, her foster parents were unwilling to provide the financial means for her to attend either of the historically Black colleges in Texas, but this "dream deferred" created a life-long desire for Mom to see her children become college graduates. Over many decades, her desire became a reality as all of her children earned college degrees or further: Two have master's degrees, and I, the eldest, have a PhD.

Mom, Dad, and Gettin' Schooled – Through College

Once upon a time I was known as Betty Lou Brown; friends used to tease me and call me BB for "Brown Bombshell," which was funny to me because I was very slim—to the point that some relatives worried that I was malnourished. "Mrs. Brown you've got a lovely daughter," went the lyrics of a song that some of my off-key boyfriends sang to me. I identified myself on all legal documents as Betty Lou Brown. By 1974, I was well established in my career as Betty Brown (forget that country-sounding Lou), and I lived the single life in the Lafayette-Orleans area of Detroit, a sort of young professional neighborhood at that time. A friend used to make a joke about my transformation from country girl to city girl: "Betty done gone Hollywoooood!" Then he strutted around my newly decorated apartment, pointing out my shiny new furniture and decorating touches.

Brown's body as buried in the plot. I recall that the family used the name "Thomas Brown" for my grandfather.

Things were really good for Betty Brown until one bright and sunny day that August a strange letter appeared in my mailbox with a San Francisco return address. It was addressed to Betty Lou Williams (my mother had been a Williams before marriage). I was twenty-seven when this happened. For my entire life my parents had told me that I did not have a birth certificate due to shoddy record-keeping practices at a poor hospital in California. Once they had finally settled in Michigan, my parents registered me for elementary school based on their verbal statements about my birth, and as time went on each successive school relied on my prior records. The appearance of my birth certificate was a surprise from my boyfriend (now husband) Michael, who knew how to apply for official records. Without my knowledge Michael sent away for my birth certificate after I confided to him that I had never seen it. He thought it would be a wonderful surprise. Well, it was a surprise – just not wonderful. This official document told me a long-held secret: I had been born out of wedlock.

To say I was shocked is to put it mildly because my parents had been obsessive about the virtue of virginity and the proper way that a young lady should act around men and boys. A "lady" did not curse, smoke, wear tight clothing, dance too close to a boy, or allow a suitor to touch more than her hand. A quick good night kiss only came *after* a prolonged period of dating for several weeks. My mother emphasized the evils of sex out of marriage through numerous and lengthy talks to me about girls who got in "trouble," meaning got pregnant out of wedlock; these talks also included repetitive and lengthy criticism of any public figure or local girl who was pregnant before or without marriage. My mother and I had argued many Sunday afternoons about the issue of a girl's virtue, and I always took the position (knowing it would get a rise out of Mom) that a girl could be virtuous, meaning a good human being, and still get pregnant out of wedlock. My father's only cautions to me about sex were voiced just before I left for college when he said, "Whatever you do, don't get pregnant. Make sure that anybody that you see treats you as well as you would treat yourself, and treat yourself well because you are worth a lot."

Thus, the disclosure of my parents' long-held secret was initially very shocking to me. I cried and moaned about their duplicity. I never spoke to my mother about this secret because I believed she was too emotionally fragile for such a discussion, or perhaps I just didn't want to make a dent in the armor of sexual propriety that she had wrapped herself in for so many years. Dad was embarrassed that the secret was out and angry that my Aunt Johnnie, whom I called immediately after opening the certificate, had told me the truth. Dad and I never spoke about his courtship of my mother or the circumstances of my conception again, but friends and family members filled in a few details of their romance after my parents died.

My father and mother met at work; Mom called herself one of the legions of "Rosie the Riveters," and Dad was a janitor. Apparently, my father had pursued my mother for years. My Aunt Johnnie recalled, "Your Dad was such a flirt and a tease— fun, charming, a rascal." He pursued Mom, revving his motorcycle up as he drove repeatedly by her rooming house, where she paid a fixed rate for the room, bath, and kitchen privileges; later he sent her love letters while he served his country aboard the U.S.S. Arkansas during WWII. Dad ultimately prevailed in his suit. I have some pictures of my parents while they were courting: Mom is slender, sepia brown, innocent, and very beautiful; Dad is lean, muscular, and masculine. One family friend called my parents' relationship "a great love story" because their chemistry lasted despite war, years of separation, and the fact that my father was already married. After my birth, my father's first wife, Ludie Brown, filed for a divorce that was granted in May 1947, and my parents married.

Neither of my parents' respective families initially approved of the liaison; this may be the reason that I did not meet my Grandmother Brown until I was in elementary school. Thus, my parents started their life together surrounded by the whispers of scandal and with few financial resources. Although the Navy honorably discharged Dad, Mother's oldest brother, Dick, told me that he had done some jail time, and he initially found it difficult to find a steady job. Perhaps this is why the young couple took jobs as live-in butler and maid and then arranged for Uncle Dick and his wife, Frankie, who had no children, to care for me until I was almost three years old.

With a second child on the way, my father ultimately found work as a factory laborer in rural southwestern Michigan near his father's farm. Dad was probably also limited in work opportunities because he had only a seventh-grade education. Over the years, Mom was frequently pregnant with what became a family of eight children. I am sure that my parents found it difficult to provide basic necessities for themselves and their brood. When she was not sick during pregnancies, Mom worked very hard to raise her children, but she did not earn money outside the home. Looking back, it seems improbable that my parents pulled 10 people out of poverty within their lifetime, but they had some help from their extended family and in turn taught us the value of a charitable nature. It was this parental impulse to generosity that was an important factor in my decision to pursue social work as a career.

My parents also taught us by example to be financially enterprising. My parents learned to grow a great deal of the food that we ate, like blueberries, raspberries, cucumbers, potatoes, carrots, peas, melons, apples, plums, green beans, and tomatoes. Dad also grew crops like rye, wheat, corn, and oats for sale or to feed our pigs, chickens, ducks, and cattle. With eight hungry children, my parents had a ready-made workforce to tend and harvest crops. Eventually these crops added significantly to our family's income. In turn my father purchased the heavy-duty equipment like tractors, plows, and hay bailers that he needed to tend all of our crops; he made even more money by hiring out on the weekends and evenings to harvest nearby neighbors' crops.

Meanwhile, my sisters and I had a little strawberry stand where we sold to passersby, especially to well-off African-American guests on vacation at the nearby Johnson's and Hodgen's resort; they came from Gary, Indiana, or Chicago to rural southwest Michigan because they were excluded by the tradition of segregation from the resorts located on Lake Michigan, where Whites from the big cities stayed. When these "city folks" happened to cruise down our dirt road in their big shiny cars every summer, they frequently bought strawberries from us kids; they liked them so much that their tips often equaled the cost of the fruit. Because money was always in short supply for allowances, we spent these profits in church, on vacations, or for treats like candy or ice cream. We also used our summer earnings for necessities like school shoes or clothing and text books.

I was thrilled when my mother taught me how to cook because I got to lick the cake batter by myself, got the first taste of the finished product and extras of anything that I made—great advantages with so much competition for food. I still take pride in my ability to cook, and unfortunately, based on my waist line, still have a voracious appetite.

I recall my mother as the first African-American militant that I ever knew. Even as a grade-school child, I knew that it was unusual for an African-American parent to challenge a White teacher. Two occasions from grade school stick out in my mind because despite my strenuous objections, Mom advocated for me. The first is when a very large White boy in black steel-toed work boots kicked me in the head when I fell while playing during recess. When I got home, my mother took one look at my face, which was bruised and twice the normal size by then. She asked me what had happened. I told her I fell and that Bobby had come over and kicked me in the head. Mom put on her white gloves, hat, nice coat, and grabbed my hand. It seemed to me that we arrived at Sheldon School within seconds of my mom getting sight of me. What she said to the teacher is burned into my mind.

"I never want to come back to this school because my child is injured on the playground." As I peeked through the keyhole in the bathroom where I was asked to stay during the conversation, I saw the teacher, an elderly White lady, draw back from my mother and reply, "Well, children are often injured outside while I am grading papers." Mom was having none of the teacher's excuse. "If my child ever comes home injured like this again, then it will be between us—you and me. You are responsible for Betty's safety, and I hold you accountable." Even though they spoke in very low tones, every word was transported through the keyhole. I fully expected the teacher to argue further and somehow to blame the situation on me. I was scared for me and for my mother. Instead, the teacher was quiet for some minutes while I smelled the dust and disinfectant surrounding me in the gloom. She said, "Thank you, Mrs. Brown, for coming in."

The teacher never punished Bobby, but he never injured me or anyone else on that playground. The next day and every day thereafter, the teacher watched the kids during recess. My mother was the first Black person that I had ever seen speak directly to a White person about a perceived injustice. She was my advocate.

The second time that Mother stood up for me was also at school; again I was sent to the dusty bathroom reeking with disinfectant and told to close the door. This time Mother had brought my book report to school, much to my embarrassment. She told the teacher, "Can you explain why Betty earned a *B* on this report?" The teacher replied, "Well, she did not completely follow the directions." Mom asked to see the directions, then asked the teacher to show her exactly what the difference was between my report and the directions. As I listened to the proper edge to my mother's voice, I sensed that Mom was not satisfied with the teacher's explanation of my grade. She asked, "Will you send the directions home with Betty so that I can read them in the future?" The teacher agreed to do so.

I recall that my mother and the teacher kept their agreement. My mother reviewed the directions for all my future reports, despite her pregnancies and housekeeping chores. I do not remember ever earning another *B* on a book report. Mom explained her actions to me at the time, "I did not see any difference between your work and the instructions. I think that teacher did not give you a higher grade because you are colored. That is not right. We will work on this."

My parents never punished us for the grades that we earned. I only recall that they might ask if we had studied, and then they discussed any difficulties we might have: Are you studying enough? Do you need a dictionary? Mother gave mild praise for report cards whether they were exceptional or mediocre. But my father lavished praise on exceptional or good report cards while offering a quarter for every *A* that we earned. My siblings and I worked for those quarters; we always wanted money for treats. But I think that I would have worked hard in school without the money because I loved school. I would cry when anything came up to prevent me from attending. School was like a magic box. There was always something in the box that I didn't know, always something new and exciting to find out about.

My parents had saved enough money by 1958 to build their dream home in rural South Haven, Michigan; this pink ranch-style house had three bedrooms, a new toilet with a shower, and a well-equipped kitchen. The house sat on twenty acres of prime blueberry property and was skirted by a pine woods, but to me the most important aspect of our new location was that I had to transfer from my one-room schoolhouse to South Haven Junior High School, a cultural shock with its three stories, gymnasium, and more than 300 students. I took a bus to school where I jostled through the halls with all manner of young folk: Jews, Catholics, Italians, and African Americans (called "colored" at the time) who had recently moved from the big cities of Chicago and Gary to the South Haven school district. There were even sons and daughters of the local merchants and politicians. The adjustment was confusing to me, and it took me until high school to get my intellectual bearings, to return to the honor roll consistently. The two most difficult parts of the transition from one-room to junior high were having male teachers (because their demeanor was so different, hence scary), and realizing that my clothing was clearly not fashionable. I often wore bulky ski pants (rummage from the relatives) topped off by thin cotton dresses. (Mom said reasonably, "You're not going to freeze, and that's what is important.")

This is why I learned to sew during junior high school. While Mom and Dad frowned on outright gifts of cash, they welcomed "in-kind gifts." That is, they were happy when relatives sent us rummage sale clothing, household items, or things that they could no longer use. Probably the most useful rummage that I received came in a huge box of assorted seasonal fabrics such as woolens and cotton prints sent by Aunt Alice and Uncle Roy Brown from New York. Mom allowed me to practice sewing with these fabrics, and with the help of my eighth-grade home economics teacher, classmates, and relatives who were quite skilled, over several years I learned to make my own clothing.

Quite capable as farmers, frugal and very practical about personal finance, my parents had absolutely no idea how to guide me through the many forms and processes necessary to apply for college and obtain a degree. Although I learned the nuts and bolts of college application from others such as my high school counselor, I knew next to nothing about college financial aid. Hence, I learned to fill out the university financial aid forms and to apply for local scholarships, but I still arrived on campus with the equivalent of a semester's expenses covered by lump-sum scholarships and loans. One fall afternoon during my first year at University of Michigan, I sat alone in the cafeteria staring at my empty tray, troubled by my lack of money for next semester when several beautiful young Black women came and sat beside me. I mumbled a hello. They asked me if there was anything wrong. Soon I spilled the story of my money problems to the sisters of Delta Sigma Theta Sorority (Karen Dobbins, Cheryl Wright, Julia Burgess, and Brendon Hudson). They were very optimistic about my chances to stay in school and gave me the telephone number and office address for the Equal Opportunity Director; according to the Deltas, this man, Dr. Robert Marion, had money for people like me who were poor with no financial resources to pay for college. The Deltas also invited me to their meetings, studied with me, and modeled the finer points of etiquette for me. Subsequently, it seemed only natural to become a member of Delta Sigma Theta Sorority because I believed they had saved me from a return to South Haven in defeat; I liked all of them, and we had fun together.

Aside from financial woes and social contacts—solved largely through my sorority association—Michigan was excruciatingly difficult. It reminded me of my journey from a one-room school house to the much-larger junior high school where I had been a hick: unfashionable and awed by the hundreds of other students. Similarly, as an undergraduate student at Michigan I had to become accustomed to vast cultural differences represented by the variety of students from different states and countries. I also lived in a dormitory where parents visited wearing matching full-length mink coats, and every morning I greeted my neighbor whose father was the founder of a Fortune 500 company. These were people whose lives I had read about in magazines. These very rich people were all White, and we never associated with each other socially. Luckily for me, my new sorority sisters welcomed me regardless of the fact that I was poor and most of them were from middle-class families; this helped me to feel that I belonged at the University of Michigan. After my financial woes were resolved, my friendships with the Deltas revolved around passing French, listening to music, going to parties, dating, learning the latest dances, and providing services to the local African-American community in Ann Arbor. This was an exciting time of my life: I studied six days a week, but on Saturdays I snapped my fingers so much that I developed calluses, and met men without a chaperone.

Even so, I would probably have flunked out of Michigan without help from two other very special Black folks. Sheila is my best friend. I almost do not remember when she wasn't my friend. Sheila is also one of my Delta sorority sisters. She came to a sorority meeting in 1966 when she transferred from Western Michigan University to University of Michigan, and we have been friends from that day to this.

I liked Sheila on first sight because she was socially assured and very hip: At the time that we met, Sheila's family still lived in Detroit where Motown was in its glory. Sheila had a fine deep-chocolate-skinned older brother who had even gone to high school with members of the Temptations. The Temptations were also some of the *super* finest men on the face of the earth then, and like most of young America, I either owned their records, tuned into television programs when they performed, listened to them on radio, attended their concerts, or danced up a funky sweat to their music. To me, from rural South Haven, her attractive brother and Detroit residence almost made my new friend a celebrity. Plus Sheila could dance really well.

Adding to Sheila's glamour were the raucous parties that she gave in the cramped apartment that she shared in University Towers on the 13th floor with three other almost-as-hip Black women. I don't know exactly how they could afford it, but Sheila and her roommates always had hot food to eat when you visited. It seemed that every good-looking (and a few who were not) athlete on Michigan's sports teams came to that apartment most nights of the week while the latest music played on the turntable in the corner, thumping out the beat for fun and flirtations. If you wanted to know who was still dating, about to break up, fighting but still in the game, free to date, or interested in the same sex, then you went to Sheila's apartment to find out. Someone there knew about virtually everything romantic within the Black student body.

Although we do not actually look alike, I believe that Sheila and I share a Black beauty aesthetic. That is, we both have nut-brown skin; our complexions have been in and out of favor in the Black community so many times during the four-plus decades of our friendship that I do not even know if we are in or out of favor now. When we first met, our complexions, round noses, full lips, and thick nappy hair meant we were out of favor as ideal Black beauties, although we were considered physically attractive because we had style, a certain ability to put the unusual together and make it work for us. We were also blessed with "big legs." A popular song at the time explained, "Don't bring me no woman with no skinny legs." So men (almost exclusively Black men during the mid-sixties) who judged a woman by more traditional Afro-centric standards, similar to the way we looked, were more likely to be attracted to us. We were always looking for Mr. Right, but I was undoubtedly more obvious as I searched in my mini-skirts or tight blue jeans and high-heeled boots. Once, for a party, I sewed myself a sleeveless pantsuit with a plunging neckline laced up with a thin gold chain; it was quite a hit. (The main difference from the way we dressed then and the dress of my current students is that we wore suggestive clothing on dates and to parties but not to classes because the dress code was "everything has a time and place.")

University of Michigan made me grow up. I knew little or nothing about suicide, drugs, alcoholism, or abortions until then. I found out a lot about life on the sprawling campus with its imposing buildings and frightening events like the gossip whispered among students and confirmed by campus news, that another student had committed suicide in a stairwell of my dormitory. These reports became routine, and once someone "helpfully" pointed out the location of a successful suicide to me in the stairwell near my room, 5414 Mary Markley Hall. I asked why anyone would do this and the answer came, "Because everyone here is used to being the best. It is what they expect of themselves, what their parents and friends expect. When folks

32

earn less than an *A,* then they feel destroyed – as though there is no reason to live." I thought that this was odd; I was happy to have a *B* or two mixed in with my *C*s. Nevertheless, in my sophomore year I too contracted the suicide bug. That is, I was not doing well in school; in fact, I was on probation for one semester. I told my mother how terrible I felt and asked her advice. As she walked away to finish dinner, she turned her head and said, "Well, dear, I am sure that a lot of people feel that way."

Looking back, I am sure that this was the best my mother could come up with, but it was an unsatisfactory answer at the time, and I was angry that my mom couldn't fix things for me. That's why I turned to Sheila with my unhappiness, and I found that she was very unhappy about school and love just like me, so we had a "pity party." One late night found us in the same dark mood, and we agreed that our lives were pretty awful. It was right after midterms; we were lonely and, miraculously, there was no one else in her apartment. We looked out of the 13th floor and spoke softly about what it would be like to be on the other side of the window pane, free to end our misery. We decided that we should go to the free psychiatric clinic the next day. To celebrate this decision we bought an alcoholic drink called "Cold Duck" and had a pizza.

While the psychiatrists were by no means a perfect solution, they did help us think through our confusion, anger at our boyfriends, and need to succeed. We plodded on and ultimately both graduated. (Many years later, I told both of my children this story while they were in adolescence so that they would know that the pressure to succeed can seem overwhelming from time to time, but that they should always turn to others such as me or their father, their friends, or a psychiatric clinic if they feel great despair.)

Between Sheila and me it is a close judgment to determine who has the most cutting and sarcastic humor. I believe Sheila wins because she can make up a poem about anything, like the mouse she found one day behind her refrigerator:

Mickey, Mickey you sure look icky
But in a pinch you'll be lunch – I'm not picky.

Aside from sharing dark moods and fun with me, Sheila gave the most informative advice about sex and love that I ever received (notwithstanding medical doctors). Because she is a year older than I, Sheila made earlier decisions on love, birth control, marriage, and children. This is why I could always ask her: "How did that feel? What is love? Did you have any side effects?" Once I fell in love the first time, I said urgently, "Where can I get a prescription for birth control pills?" Sheila told me and I took care of that problem pronto. Sheila said, "I don't know" very rarely. When she did, then she would also tell me, "You should ask your doctor." Her advice on things sensual and sexual has always been accurate and wise.

I never had a big sister; everyone in my family depended on me to make the first and correct steps into maturity. If I had a big sister, then I hope she would be as wonderful to me as my friend and sorority sister, Sheila.

An African-American teaching fellow also gave me a hand up; he was the only educator of my race that I had from elementary school through college. Mr. Jergenson was physically round—not fat, but not at all like the chiseled athletes that I dated—with caramel-colored skin and a bushy black mustache. He told our class that he had graduated from Harvard; the only other Harvard graduates I had ever heard of at the time were President John Kennedy and members of his family. Mr. Jergenson's stock as a teacher went to the top of my chart. He could do no wrong.

Mr. Jergenson threw me a lifeline as an intellectually naïve undergraduate. *Ego, id,* and *superego,* key terms in psychology, were fanciful words to me, and the ideas they matched seemed even stranger. His essay assignment to use these concepts proved fateful. Looking back, I realize that he called me into his office for a conference about my assignment because I had not used these concepts correctly even though he gave me a low *B* grade. I was flattered by the extra attention from a Harvard grad, so when he cleared his throat and explained, "I want to help you with these concepts because your paper reflects an unusual understanding of this material, one that is outside of use in my field," I was pleased rather than insulted or upset and eagerly accepted his additional explanation of how to use the concepts. Mr. Jergenson suggested that I return to review other assignments before I submitted them, and although I did not get an *A* in introductory psychology, I did leave the class with confidence that I understood the basic ideas.

After this positive experience with Mr. Jergenson, I began to seek further explanations about content whenever I had questions in my other classes; usually such conferences helped me with my grade and understanding.

One day as I sat in Mr. Jergenson's tiny office recovering from the climb up the steep dusty stairs, he looked through his large round glasses at me to ask, "Would you like to take an independent study class with me this spring?" I replied, "What is that?" He explained, "It's a class that you and I design. Since you have been coming along so well in the introductory class, I thought it might help you to understand more about the practical application of psychological concepts if you can go with me to one of my practice sites, the Whitmore Lake Boys Training School, where I consult on Tuesday evenings. We could figure out a project that you could do there while I consult, and I could give you a ride out there. It's about a half hour from here. I have several other students who will be going." I trusted Mr. Jergenson—Carl now—because he told me that all of the students going out to Whitmore Lake would call him by his first name. I had already learned a lot from him, so I said, "Sure."

"Sit your ass down." I had to explain to the two boys who towered over me at 6' tall and 200 lean muscular pounds each. Much later I realized that the boys were potentially dangerous, but at the time it never even occurred to me that at 130 pounds and 5'7" I might have been outmatched physically. I just knew that I would not allow fighting to interrupt our group work. Carl had told me that for my independent study I could hold a meeting with some of the boys incarcerated at the facility for about 60 minutes while he and the other students worked in another part of the sprawling locked-down collection of buildings that looked much like a small community college campus. An important difference was that these students could not escape classes over the 12-foot high wire fences watched by guards. My meetings focused on drama when I realized that I could use some of the same exercises I learned each week in my college drama class at Michigan with my group of boys. I think that the boys attended because there was little else for them to do; during the first few weeks we all got along very well. In the forty years since, I have never cussed in professional situations at clients, but at Whitmore Lake Boys Training School the words just leaped out of my mouth. As the oldest of eight, I was used to bossing younger kids around; my younger brothers were bigger and stronger than I, but I didn't fear them. Surprisingly, as I stood up between the two potential combatants and stared at them, they parted and then moved slowly back to their chairs, showing their reluctance with lack of speed.

I explained to the entire group as the two potential fighters sulked, "Look, we all want to have a little fun here, but if there is a fight it will ruin it for everyone. The supervisor here and my teacher will not let me come back once you start a fight" (which was probably true). "If we just keep on doing these exercises together then you can come here each week and have a little fun rather than stay in your unit all the time." Everyone bought this logic, and there was never another argument while I was at the school.

Later, the supervisor of the unit told me, "If you ever need a recommendation for social work, then I will write it because you handled yourself really well." Although Carl wanted me to learn more about psychology and called what I did at Whitmore Lake

Boys Training School psycho-drama, it seemed to have no relationship to the class that I had taken with him. Yet as the supervisor, a tall African-American gentleman named Ralph, explained more about social group work to me, I became very interested. Ralph pointed out that helping the teens to learn how to interact with each other based on their common interest was called social group work. He told me the classes I would need to take as an undergraduate and suggested that I might also want to consider graduate school in the profession. I asked Ralph with wonder, "People get paid for this?" He reared his six-foot-five frame backwards and let out a long laugh that seemed to roll up from his toes as he rocked toward me and said, "Not only do they get paid, but many of them would be proud to handle themselves as well as you do now. Honey, let me tell you that you've got talent. So yes, what you are doing is actually a job that people get paid for. It's called social work."

Although Carl was very disappointed when I explained to him that social work rather than psychology seemed like the profession for me, he gave me an *A* for my independent study class.

When I reflect on this first social work experience, I realize that it was very dangerous and that I was very lucky. With absolutely no training I had been left alone with a group of delinquent boys in a room without a guard or means to call a guard. Ralph and the other evening staff circulated throughout the multiple floors of the unit, so I did not always have immediate back-up if things turned violent. I later found that while some of the young men were at the facility for chronic truancy from school, others had committed much more serious crimes such as assault. Currently (2013) social work students are only allowed to do such work after an extensive background check, interview, orientation, safety training, under supervision, and often in view of a closed-circuit camera. I was lucky in many ways.

A Mentor Makes it Happen: Undergraduate to Graduate School

As a junior in college, I applied for summer employment as a research assistant in the School of Social Work. This successful application led me to a first-generation doctoral student, Claire Lanham, who became a long-term mentor. Soon after we met, Claire, a tiny, fearless White lady in three-inch heels who spoke with a distinctive Tennessee twang, told me that she wanted me to understand how social services worked in Detroit.[3] From that point on, she both lectured and quizzed me about the anti-poverty services we were evaluating. She introduced me to other important service institutions in the city like Detroit Receiving Hospital that cared for the poor. Often Claire would ask me, "What do you think will happen to that person once they are referred (to a specific service)?" I would take a wild guess, and then Claire would gently offer her own correct assessment. Claire said, "I think you would be a great social worker (one of my undergraduate majors) so I am going to make sure to explain how all these services work. You have wonderful skills of observation, and I believe if you understand the city, the services, and the eligibility criteria then you will be able to work here if you choose. I know you are from a rural area just like me, and that is why you need to learn this city in order to be competitive for jobs here."

Claire kept in contact with me after the summer job was over. She came to my graduation, met my family, and urged me to apply for graduate school even though I was very reluctant. "Betty, you should go ahead and apply for any jobs that you are interested in. Meanwhile, if you fill out this graduate school application form for University of Michigan, then I will pay your application fee. In the end, you can compare the amount of

---

[3] At the end of this chapter are suggestions on how to make the most of the mentorship experience.

money you might get from a scholarship to the amount that you get from your job offers. I would be happy to write you a letter of reference, and I am sure that some of the other faculty researchers would too." Her offer impressed me because I knew that Claire could ill afford the $25 fee since she had a disabled husband and five minor children. I was admitted to graduate school on a traineeship that paid for full tuition and provided me with a monthly stipend. By comparison my job offers were so low that they basically matched the financial package offered by the graduate school. I did not know a lot about how to handle money at the time, but I knew that I would have more earning power after a graduate degree.

For me the greatest challenges of graduate school revolved around wrestling with the impulse to fix things for my clients according to my own insights and time line. Because I had taken a second major in social work as an undergrad, the content was very familiar, interesting, but not too difficult to grasp. However, when I went to my social work internships, I found that I needed more than the assertiveness and goodwill I had shown at Whitmore Lake Boys Training School to be effective with the clients. For example, I had several teens in an after-school group who were labeled by the agency as mentally retarded, the term used in the early 1970s. My insight, gained in 22 years of life, told me that the members of this group—all African American— used the label to get out of schoolwork, and that they had not been exposed to any alternatives. To fix their problem I proposed a field trip in my car to visit the University of Michigan.

In supervision, my wise professor helped me to see some of the errors in my approach. She suggested, "Find out what the teens think their problems might be and how *they* would like to address them. Then, find out what resources the agency has for their solution." This advice worked not only for the teens in my group, but also for most professional social work situations that I have been in since then; we now call my supervisor's advice empowerment. (At Eastern Michigan University I once taught an entire class to master's students around this idea that requires the worker to put aside his or her own judgment about what is good for clients and to find out the clients' own goals and desires and then match them with agency resources.) When I followed through with my supervisor's advice, I found that the teens in my group were bored with the lack of daily intellectual stimulation in their curriculum. Matching this problem to agency resources and procedures then became my challenge, rather than finding a way to take them on a field trip to the University of Michigan in my car. It took the remainder of my internship to help the teens achieve a small change in their curriculum.

From this and other graduate school internship experiences, I began to get a glimmer of my future aspirations to become an administrator. While I did learn to be effective and help clients make small changes, I started to understand that I really wanted to help agencies, neighborhoods, and society to achieve large-scale changes.

While I matured as a young social worker, I also learned a painful romantic lesson.

Michael, my husband of more than 35 years, says he is very grateful that the man I intended to marry during graduate school broke our engagement. My fiancé, Roland, was a traditional man. He wanted a woman who would be a credit to him in social situations, a good housewife, and mother to his children. We were young and very hot for each other so we thought that was love and that love would conquer any differences we might have.

"You can have some input into our family decisions, but I will always have veto power. I can't have a wife who will substitute her judgment for mine or who will compete with me in the workforce," announced Roland while we stood among an assortment of couches and end tables one summer evening. I laughed and said, "You must be kidding? I'm not going to be a second fiddle in our marriage." We had dated for two years prior, met the parents and siblings, purchased the ring, and were planning our home. He had just begun a career in business after finishing graduate school; I thought that our future would be financially secure with two incomes to rely upon. I was twenty-four, and he was the only man that I had known intimately.

We faced off in the middle of the furniture store growling at each other. "I thought you knew I wanted a career, Roland. Why else would I suffer through undergraduate and graduate school?" I said as tears sprang to my eyes, and I realized that he might even believe what he said. He squinted, flexed his biceps, puffed out his chest, and planted his feet—looking just like a bull ready to withstand the charge of a matador—then answered, "So that you can be a good helpmate to me, of course. You will stay home and take care of our children." I responded as though I were breathing fire, "Well, that is not going to happen—it is a waste of my education. It's a waste of all the agony and money that I have put into it." At that point the sales clerk began walking briskly toward us, but took one look at our faces and body language and turned quickly away.

The sad drama that was the end of my first romance played out over a couple of months. Each of us repeated our positions after making love, after a movie, after a good dinner, even after a visit to a counselor; but we could not find a compromise. I walked away from Roland with four realizations about me and men. One, I had to be an equal partner in all marital decisions; two, I wanted a career; and three, I wanted to have children. The fourth realization was probably the most important. I could believe that I loved someone, but love would not be enough reason for me to marry him. If I ever married, my mate and I would need to share the same vision for our future.

Study Questions

Although I was unaware of it at the time, my parents not only told us how to behave, but they also modeled the behaviors of industry and thrift. They were ashamed of their romance and did not want me to follow their lead in that instance, but in the end my conception had no impact on my life course.

1. What family secrets have affected you? How have you dealt with them?
2. In our society how does the marital status, race, sex, or sexual orientation of a parent relate to the child? Is your opinion reflected in social policy? If so how? If not, why not? Would you like to see this changed?
3. If you are a college student, how do you seek others with similar values and aspirations such as occurred for me with the Deltas at University of Michigan?
4. How do you expect to balance romance and commitment with a career?
5. As someone who has benefitted enormously from wonderful mentors, here are some rules I learned that I wish someone had told me long ago.

Your Mentor Is Not Your Mama:
Things Your Mentor Wants You to Know

---

1. Remember that ***Your Mentor Is Not Your Mama.*** That is, your mentor is not related to you and does not owe you anything. Ideally, your mentor will be dedicated to you in direct proportion to your effort to prove that you are worthy of their time and energy; this is unlike your Mama who will love you through "thick and thin," many times without expecting anything in return and putting up with some of your less desirable behaviors.

2. Like other voluntary relationships (friends and lovers), mentors are only likely "to be with you" if you are pleasant and reciprocal; don't drag them down with drama and complaints. Therefore, as you plan your career and higher education, do everything you can to meet their expectations. Some examples: if the mentor asks you to meet a deadline for a chapter or hearing, and you can do it only by moving heaven and earth, then move heaven and earth to meet that deadline.

3. If you have any difficulties with deadlines, and try not to, then you must let mentors know beforehand. Do not show up on the due date with nothing in hand; this is a waste of the mentor's precious time. Better yet, send your material to the mentor a day or two prior to your deadline so they have the opportunity to review it before the meeting.

4. As a rule, mentors work with students because they enjoy your area of study, so share new information, theories, facts, and findings with the mentor as soon as possible.

5. Although you are not able to choose **Your Mama,** you are able to choose your mentor. Therefore, choose wisely. Begin your search for a mentor based upon how similar their research is to your area of interest. You can find out more about their work by looking on the school or department website or through a search of library indexes in your field. You can also ask your high school teachers or undergraduate professors if they have any recommendations for a mentor at schools that you may wish to attend.

6. When you are shopping around for a mentor, ask other students about the mentor's reputation. Are they dependable? How long has it taken for most of their students to graduate? Do they remember deadlines and file paper work timely? Do they support their student's interests?

7. Unlike **Your Mama,** a mentor's time for you is limited. They often have consulting work that may pay from $1,000-5,000 per day, so always respect their time. Be punctual, but do not take offense if the mentor is late. Mentors may also have classes to prepare for, papers to grade, committees to attend, and emails to infinity. Give the respect due to someone who has walked where you walk and further (think senior scholar).

8. Finally, if the mentor becomes your thesis or dissertation chairperson, allow that person to give their input. (Who will be part of your committee? When is a good time to defend your work?) You can always recommend individuals and schedules to the mentor, but remember that the dissertation chairperson or thesis advisor knows more than you. **Unlike Mama,** mentors in this role do not have to honor your choices in life.

Chapter 4 — Family Matters: Walking the Path, Family, and the Achievement Gap

"Will I lose touch with my family if I go on for a degree?" For those of us who are the first generation to attend college, there is a realistic fear that any educational achievement will become a wedge between us and family members. We have a great potential for educational achievement (high school, college, a graduate degree, or the doctorate), but we are afraid that the achievement and its financial rewards might open a gap between us, our friends, and family members. We know that as we advance there will be fewer people like us. So it stands to reason that to attain a degree—especially a doctorate—can make us so different from the majority of all Americans, including our family, that we will not fit in. The fear is: I will lose those that I love; I will be different and lonely.

We can still love and be loved even though we will be different from our family and many friends; we don't have to be lonely. Having a doctoral degree by definition almost always means that we have discovered something very few other people know or can understand, so it stands to reason that our family and friends may not be able to discuss our work with us. Instead, family members may express jealousy of our potential or fear of losing us when they say, "Why are you still going to school?" Another challenge that first-generation doctorates will likely have is introduction to a culture which is at odds with the one where we were raised. This new cultural life style will involve different rules concerning what it means to be polite, clothes that may appear boring to us, strange music or art works we are unfamiliar with, and a sense of morality that revolves almost exclusively around the individual's desire to get ahead. Further, unless we make bad financial choices, we will have a lot more income, wealth, and possessions than others in our birth-family. So as a result of our academic achievement, we are very likely to become a member of the financial, social and intellectual elite, the upper class. Some in our family may even see us as a "sell-out," one of the enemies of poor and working folk.

This fear of an achievement gap bothered me, so along the way I came up with some ways to stay close to my family and old friends (none of whom had the doctorate). Some things worked well and others things failed.

Husband and the PhD

"Isn't it really difficult to sleep with your wife now that she's an assistant dean and doctoral student at the most prestigious school of social work in the country?" A friend asked my husband (who had just earned his Master of Business Administration), shortly after I enrolled at the University of Chicago.

Michael sarcastically responded, "No, she's the same old country girl that I married from South Haven, Michigan. She was throwing mules then—that's still her greatest talent."

Although Michael considerably overestimated my physical strength, his comment made me think more about my supposedly "high-class" promotion to assistant dean and doctoral student status in light of where I came from—a working farm where we had livestock. I also recalled that when I was a teenager, the animals' manure stench, ripened by heat in the blaze of seasonal sun but mercifully tamed in the winter, had really undercut my confidence to flirt with some of the neighborhood boys. Another "farm" memory is burned into the "hard drive" of my memory file. I had come home during an undergraduate college break and one of our 200-pound pigs escaped to the sidewalk in front of our house. The pig timed its leisurely stroll past our large picture window just as I showed off for a family photograph wearing a very expensive outfit that I shouldn't have purchased on credit. So Michael's response to our friend helped me to stay grounded as a "girl" who had been raised on a farm (with lots of stinking manure) and who had been brought to her senses long ago by a very large pink pig when she tried to "put on airs" to be something that she was not.

Pigs became my personal mascot. Shortly after I had these recollections, I began to collect and display pigs in my university office. I had lots and lots of pigs: crystal, iron, porcelain, plastic, silver, glass, brass, wood, rubber, and plush toy. They remain, more than thirty years later, a daily reminder that I am "just a farm girl."

"Truth be told," as some of my church members used to say, Michael did wonder what would happen to our marriage once I started the doctoral program. As Michael and I relaxed in each other's arms in our darkened bedroom a few weeks before my first class, he asked me, "Won't you meet someone else who is really handsome and smart at the University of Chicago, and that guy will take you away from me?" At the time I sarcastically joked, "Oh, of course not, honey. Most of them look like toads. Even the ones who are handsome were the 'nerds' or intellectually absorbed and socially inept of their high school and college classes. They haven't become more charming since then." I can be somewhat flirtatious; Michael and I agree that we are married but not dead. This means that we both appreciate other physically attractive people. But during my journey to obtain a doctorate at Chicago, there just was no one who fit Michael's description. Most important, there was no one who was as good a match for me—even temporarily—as my husband.

My Delta sorority sister from University of Michigan days and best friend, Sheila Malone, tells me all the time: "Girl, I don't know what that man has got, but whatever it is you should bottle it and sell it." On Sunday, January 25, 2004, the *Detroit Free Press* ran a story titled, "Sexy is as sexy does," where I tried to explain my ongoing love for and attraction to my husband:

> Being sexy sometimes does include looks, and Michael Chappell 57, of Canton, who was nominated by his wife, Betty Brown-Chappell, has them. That's gravy for a wife who also is grateful for her family man: 'We have been married for 28 years, and he still brings me flowers and tells me I'm beautiful despite middle-age sags, bags, wrinkles and gray hair,' wrote Brown-Chappell, 57. 'When I look at him I am attracted not only by 6-feet-5 inches of fine brown real estate, but also by the strength of character necessary to be a father to our two children who reached maturity quite successfully. Their success (one is a Big Ten scholar athlete and the other one a doctoral candidate) is a tribute to his patience (even when angry), dedication (in the face of career obligations) and affection (even during the teen years). He is a singular figure in my life.
>
> He is sexy when he envelopes me in his arms each night after we've both had a hard day's work – a safe harbor. I especially enjoy that safe harbor on chilly nights when he warms my cold skin with his hot body – that is sexy. Despite the decades together and years past, I know that I will never know him completely. He is still a man of mystery. I only realized this summer that he is shy!' (as cited in Riley, 2004)

Michael amuses and amazes me. He has a wicked and profane sense of humor (think love child of Chris Rock and Bill Cosby) that makes me laugh so hard that sometimes I rock back on my heels, as I cry and choke for air because of something he has said about someone. His favorite people to pick on are politicians. He is adventurous where I am more reserved about hobbies like jet-skiing or parasailing. We have both tried some rather unusual things; for example, we walked sixty miles to raise money for breast cancer services, treatment, and research. Alternatively, we also enjoy some rather ordinary but fun things; we like to garden, play card games, dance, and go to the theatre.

Yet it would be dishonest if I did not admit that Michael and I have had some hard times, as I am sure all long-term couples have. We got married in our late twenties—a little ancient for the times—and set up house. This required us to join our families, finances, households, temperaments, and habits. The first test: Could we get along with all of the new challenges that swirled around us? We mostly managed. We both soon grew to cherish and love our respective sets of in-law parents and were deeply affected many years later when they departed this world. Thus, one potential wedge between couples was resolved early on.

A second potential wedge, finances, remains an ongoing issue. From the first day of marriage, we decided to maintain separate finances and to have a joint household account. Through trial and error plus some shut-off notices, we concluded that I would be the person responsible to pay our bills and taxes; this has worked for many decades. More recently, our financial advisor, Paul, tried during the last ten years to pound it into our heads that we are one financial unit both legally and practically. When retirement decisions had to be made, we relented to Paul and began to plan our investments together—mostly. We have resisted Paul's perspective because neither of us ever wanted to be financially dependent on the other, so we sort of played tag on investments and savings: When I saw Michael with a fat retirement plan, I tried to fatten mine up; when I started college accounts for both children, Michael took the baton from me for Aisha's account; if I contributed to my family's support, then he soon offered to do the same. Thankfully, neither of us has wildly different financial goals, and we decided that we each had to agree to divert our joint resources, like a credit card or mortgage, to fund our graduate degrees (an MBA for him and the PhD for me). To maintain a joint place of comfort on how to manage money has taken every day of the last thirty-seven years; we never stop negotiating, sharing, and comparing ways to do things better.

The first night of our life together when we officially joined our households was spent in the bedroom of our new three-story condominium in downtown Detroit surrounded by boxes and bags piled to the ceiling. We had split the down payment and all the fees. Michael, Mr. MBA, says all real estate is just your best guess about how well your home will sell once the time comes; if you make a profit, then it was a good decision. Over the years as we bought and sold three homes, we have continued to make good real estate decisions because we have profited with each sale. However, 709 South Harvey in tree-lined Oak Park, Illinois, was a lousy decision on a place to live with two young children. It had such large holes in the basement foundation—discovered the month before we sold it fourteen years later—that we had a constant fight with vermin such as squirrels, Super Rat, roaches, and mice. (Michael told me not to include anything about Super Rat in this book because we will seem unclean; but Super Rat got what he deserved, so I think it is a good story.) Super Rat disrupted my doctoral studies one bright Sunday morning about 6 a.m. as he ate through the heavy plastic garbage can in our kitchen. We tried everything to kill him: glue traps, metal traps, poison, and an exterminator. Finally, one afternoon our housekeeper, Mrs. Raggs, and the children discovered Super Rat glued to the floor under our kitchen oven. He probably died of old age.

We have joined our temperaments, but there continue to be road bumps. Here are three examples. First, I have learned to be quieter, not to chatter on incessantly, and Michael has accommodated my need to verbally express almost every emotion or idea that I have ever had by becoming an even more attentive listener. Because of our ongoing dialog, I believe that he

50

has the equivalent of his doctorate since I told him every excruciating idea and fact so many times that I am sure he memorized it. A second example deals with how we differ in our standards of cleanliness; he cleans when he can see his foot prints in the shower. I clean on a schedule. We compromised on this; we each have our own bathroom. Areas where guests are welcome should be cleaned on schedule, but the family room is "lived in." Finally, we also maintain separate office spaces, and neither of these areas is neat. His secret: Most of the time you cannot open the door and walk from one wall to the other in my husband's home office because of the numerous desks, boxes, files, stacks of papers, and computers. My secret: I routinely hire people to help me file and sort every other year or so, plus I donate and give away lots of stuff.

So we continue to muddle along as we celebrate each day that we are still together to have a partner who shares joys and sorrows.

Family of Origin, the PhD and the Achievement Gap

Dad, Benjamin Franklin Brown

One day when I was eighteen years old and planned to shop in a nearby town for college with my summer savings—not the best financial idea—my father surprised me when he asked if I would meet him for a donut afterwards. This was a strange request to me because I could rarely recall a conversation with my father unless the other children or my mother were also present, and our family did not have much extra money to spend at a restaurant. Curious and a little afraid that I had unwittingly done something wrong, I agreed to meet my father for coffee and a donut.

As we settled into our seats at the tiny glass-walled donut shop, I looked over at my dad, who was dressed in his usual heavy denim work clothes despite the heat. This was way before denim became the American uniform and cost an arm and a leg. Although I squirmed around on the sticky leatherette chair trying to find a position that was less sweaty, Dad seemed unusually calm. He had a serious but kindly look on his sun-darkened face and his hands, grown massive over the decades of labor at his two jobs, farming and molding automobile parts, were crossed and still. After we received our order, I waited to hear what he had to say.

"Betty, I know that throughout your childhood you have seen me as a disciplinarian, the person who spanked you and corrected you whenever you did something that your mother or I thought was wrong. "

I nodded yes to this point as I painfully recalled many spankings that Dad had given me as a young kid or whippings with the thick black leather razor belt as I got older. We were punished physically for lying, hitting siblings, or stealing. I also unhappily remembered Dad's loud shouts and baritone bellows about "acting stupid" when I dragged my feet to do a chore, back-talked (used a disrespectful tone of voice, argued, or made a rude comment to either parent), or tried to swish my hips when I walked into the front room when my boyfriends came to pick me up. Equally painful to recall were the many times Dad bellowed at me on an early Saturday morning to "get your lazy butt out of bed and clean this house, and help your mother."

Now Dad looked down into his coffee, then made eye contact with me, and continued almost meekly, "What you don't know is that often after I spanked you I went to my bedroom and cried too."

I said a little too loudly, as the waitress turned to check on us, "What?"

Dad continued, "Your mother and I decided when we had children that my role would be as disciplinarian, and that is what I did, but I never enjoyed it. To hurt one of my children hurt me too. Yes, I often cried after I spanked you, but I did what I believed was best for you to learn to be a good person, what I believed was best for all of you kids. What I want you to know now is that I consider you to be an adult because you are leaving for college; you will make your own decisions, and you will not depend on me for financial support or for a home. I want to be your friend."

My mouth hung open in shock and disbelief. What my father said to me was the exact opposite impression that I had of him for my entire life. It seemed to me that the deal he had with my mother placed him in the terrible position of almost always being the "bad guy" with us kids, and my mother traded on this impression. During the difficult times of my parents' marriage, frequently before and after the birth of another child, my mother had characterized Dad to me and later to my siblings as "a mean man." For evidence she would point to the most recent whipping that he had given me, or she might recall marital arguments which she had with Dad that were often in my hearing, and she spoke at length about his tone of voice or mean phrases. Sometimes she would follow this list of complaints with a plan to take us kids and leave my father to return to live in Evanston, Illinois, to be with her family or friends. Mom acted on this only once, and the event ended up more as a week-long enjoyable vacation where relatives took us to fun places and fed us great food. When we returned home, both of my parents were happy. Unfortunately, I kept the original harsh words in the back of my mind for my entire childhood, and my mother could rekindle my negative feelings about my father very easily.

This request—to be my friend—also butted up against traits that I still share with my father. One is being "frank." This trait is somewhat offset with kindness and generosity—sometimes to a fault—but when we perceive that "someone done us wrong," then some very cutting statements might be uttered in counterattack. To be frank also meant we would tell the truth to family and friends without any tact. For example, my father sometimes called me pretty when I was dressed for church, but he might just as easily point out that I had really big feet—or, as he put it, "Real big understandings." Recently, one of my brothers stated that his feelings had been hurt when I told him half-jokingly that he had he had a fat head. Many relatives, including my husband and children, fondly remember my father because of his ability to coin funny and unusual phrases, but living with that, especially when boyfriends came to visit, was not so funny or endearing.

There were some things on the plus side of my thoughts about Dad. I also recalled the instances where his more "friendly" side had emerged during childhood. Dad called himself a "Jack of All Trades." I believe that this phrase included not only the skills (trades) he had learned in the navy, barbering and cooking, but also the artistic abilities that helped him to design and build our first home and several barns plus spend time explaining to me how and why he painted pictures in oil or carved statues. Perhaps most memorable were the many games and sports that I had enjoyed with Dad such as tennis, bicycling, archery, volleyball, softball, checkers, poker, Monopoly, and Chinese checkers, to name a few. Because we lived in a rural area, often unreachable for days even by snow plows, we were often confined to the house as we looked out the window to see six feet high snow drifts circle our house. At such times, the indoor games were a welcome diversion to what could have become several very dull days of forced hibernation.

Trying to get a grip on this new reality of "adulthood and friendship," I took a few more bites of my chocolate covered donut—which was really good—as I chewed on my father's request. I hoped that this would be a friendship with the "Jack of All Trades" aspect of his personality. I said, "Sure, Dad. I am just so surprised about how you felt all these years."

As I completed my undergraduate degree, then the Master of Social Work, started a career and sought the doctoral degree, I found in my dad a "senior" friend who offered advice only on rare occasions and who listened intently about my life. We also spoke about the family farm, money issues, family news, my college classes, and later doctoral research and employment. I would often come home and sit near the brick fireplace where a fire roared, especially in the winter, as Dad leaned back in his favorite over-stuffed red reclining chair to ask, "Well, little girl, what are you studying now?" Dad, with his grammar-school education, would listen intently and then ask for more information about the classes or the progress of my research. Often he would relate something I said to current events. He never got tired of hearing about my education or career accomplishments, and he had a great recall for topics we had discussed in the past so he sometimes asked me for an update on them. One of our few disagreements was on how to diaper my children and then how to discipline them. I think he figured that as the father of eight, he had the greater knowledge in those areas.

A couple years before my father was diagnosed with the cancer that ultimately killed him, he took me aside and said, "Little girl, you better finish this degree because I want to be alive when you graduate. You just never know." He was 74 at the time, and his statement helped push me to get my doctorate finished.

Thus, the comment I treasured most at my graduation came from my father. Wearing a black velvet doctoral beret and dressed in the flowing bright maroon and black velvet doctoral robe and shawl that was the required uniform of the day, I swept down the stairs of the massive stone Rockefeller Chapel into the sunlight as a new "doctor." I turned and saw Dad and Mom as they stood in the shade of a tiny maple tree; it was very hot, and they crowded under the little shade that this upper crust environment had created from the decades of profits made by Rockefeller's oil companies. [4] My dad had recently had cancer

---

[4] John D. Rockefeller founded Standard Oil during the late 1800s; with some of the proceeds he founded University of Chicago and was instrumental in many other nationally recognized charitable causes. A Rockefeller still sits on the board that governs of the university; the family maintains its wealth and among other assets holds a major interest in J. P. Morgan Chase Bank.

surgery and could not wear a dress suit to the ceremony. Instead, he had on a beige linen uniform jump suit because he could fit his colostomy bag under it. Beside him Mom, now in her late sixties, stood looking somewhat stooped and wore a beige lace dress which had seen better days; on her feet were thick brown sandals instead of her usual high heels. I am ashamed to say that my first thought was, "They don't fit in here." Just then my father looked over at me as he moved from the tiny shade of the tree into the blistering sun to say, "You are one smart little girl." I realized at that moment that my parents *did fit in* because without them I would not be present either. Without them, I would not be able to fully appreciate the distance my achievement had brought all of us, from farm land to the fantastic beauty of Rockefeller Chapel. I think because he only had a seventh grade education, my dad probably understood more than anyone else how far my achievement had taken our family.

Mother, Clara Lucille Brown

I was probably seven years old when I heard a piercing scream that meant the end of my carefree childhood. The scream, a woman's that I groggily came to recognize as my mother's, woke me from a deep sleep to peer into the darkness of the single room that I shared with my two younger sisters, Gail and Frances. Soon the screams were followed by crying. I overheard my parents' conversation, and learned that my mother's brother, Horace, had died unexpectedly in his mid-thirties in Waco, Texas. As the sun rose, my parents made hasty preparations to drive the thousands of miles between rural Michigan where we lived to Waco, Texas, for the funeral. An older lady friend of the family, Mrs. Kenner, agreed to stay with us children. As my mother kissed us goodbye I could tell from her swollen face that she was very sad; my dad tried to comfort her. Then he turned to me and said, "Betty you watch out for your sisters and help Mrs. Kenner take care of them. Okay?" Then my parents were gone, toting along the youngest baby who still nursed, to attend a funeral for someone I was related to but had never met, someone whom Mother obviously loved a great deal and from whose death she would never quite recover.

Up until this time in the mid 1950s, Mother had been a cheerful although frequently pregnant woman. One of my fondest memories of childhood was the Friday afternoon story time with Mother. My father would do our weekly grocery shopping after he got paid on Fridays, and he always bought us a book that belonged to a collection known as the Little Golden Books; I think they were called this because they had gold glitter spines and accents on the illustrated covers. So Friday afternoons were a double treat: We almost always had store-bought cookies and fresh creamy milk while Mother read us the newest golden-book fairy tale. We were transported into the adventures of Cinderella, Snow White, Br'er Rabbit, or the Three Little Kittens. I never tired of these stories because it seemed so magical to me that reading could take you to an entirely new and strange existence. Like all children, we asked for Mom to read the stories again and again until my father purchased the next book.

The Golden Books were a special pleasure to us in our rural setting where there was no public library; for a long time the one-room school library's major stock was a set of encyclopedias and a dictionary. Eventually, the county had a vehicle called a "Bookmobile" which was filled with hundreds of books for all ages; it circulated to the rural schools monthly.

Dirt was my mother's greatest enemy. Most of the week, it seemed that my mother was always busy cleaning our house. For a number of years, my parents slept in a room that doubled as the dining room during the day while my sisters and I slept in the living room on rollaway beds that folded up and were covered during the day. She developed a reputation as one of the best housekeepers and cooks in the neighborhood and indeed in the entire extended family. She would assign me and my little sisters chores such as putting the dishes away or clearing the table, but initially we were too young to be much help. Hence, the bulk of the housekeeping fell to Mom: She cooked, swept, dusted, washed on a manual ringer, hung the clothes outside to dry, and then starched and ironed them. In addition to this routine, she helped Dad to harvest crops as they ripened, and then canned them in the fall for winter. Although Mother helped out with the cash crops, her particular talent was all for show. She asked Dad to plant flowers that she cultivated for their beauty: perennials like roses, lilacs, lilies, or iris which would be complimented by marigolds, dahlias, and assorted other annual plants. There was little need to water, because there always seemed to be enough rain. The flowers provided the one unqualified pleasurable exception to Mother's mighty war on dirt.

There were many sources of dirt and grime. We had a coal-burning furnace that emitted clouds of fine soot as it burned in late fall, winter, and early spring. The soot rose to the ceiling and had to be brushed down with a dust rag and broom almost weekly. Of course, spring and summer presented Mom with special housekeeping challenges because we did not have sidewalks or a paved driveway for the first fourteen years of my life; everyone constantly tracked dirt into the house, and it turned to mud whenever there was rain. To make matters worse, as kids we were fascinated with mud, and we played in it whenever we could sneak and do it before Mom's eagle eyes caught us squishing our feet in the cool puddles or stirring mud pies. Even the dry season of August had its own way of thwarting Mom's quest for cleanliness: Passing cars stirred up billows of dust from the unpaved dirt road in front of the house for her to wash out of our lacy curtains or sweep from the floor.

Many decades after Mother's war on dirt and grime ceased, my cousin Toni Brownlee paid her a compliment: "I thought of Aunt Lucille as the perfect mother, like on television, because she kept such a clean home, she was so beautiful, and you all were always so well cared for." During my first years of life my mother seemed to enjoy her work; I recall that she would sometimes sing as she prepared our meals, and it was always a church song. I seem to remember her bare flat feet, like mine, planted on the floor in front of the sink as she washed dishes and sang a jolly tune like "This little light of mine."

However, once my parents returned from the grim business of burying Uncle Horace in Texas, it seemed that the light went out of Mom's life for many years. I have heard Mom's state of mind called "situational depression." That is a deep sadness, lack of joy, and unresponsiveness to daily activities and routines. Perhaps this latest death reminded her that she had suffered the loss of her father, grandmother, and mother all by the age of fourteen. In later life she would excuse herself from visiting me if I became ill by recalling how hard sickness was for her to handle. It seemed to conjure up a childhood memory of when she had been required to sit up overnight with her grandmother's dead body before the funeral. Perhaps in this context, it is understandable that the death of her brother might cause her to revisit all her other losses and to become despondent or depressed. She lost so much weight that none of her clothes fit. She slept most of the day, and then was restless during the night. She could not carry out all the household chores, and Mrs. Kenner often came to help out.

Soon I was enlisted to help. Over the remaining years of my childhood I gradually learned to wash dishes satisfactorily, to cook for the family, and to keep house with my mother's standard. I was put in charge of my younger siblings. At first I did not perform these tasks well, but I learned to check with my parents as I worked, and they guided me so that one day Dad said, "You are really a big help." My father took Mom to the doctors repeatedly, but she returned from these expensive visits (patients paid all medical costs at this time) even more unhappy, and groggy. This last was probably from the prescription tranquilizers that were the only medication her doctor gave to her for emotional problems. Thus, she was bedridden. Finally, my mother's brother, sisters, and friends traveled from Illinois on a sunny Sunday afternoon to see if they could be of help. This was a turning point because Uncle Dick, Mother's oldest brother, said that if she could not regain her health in rural Michigan, then the family wanted to take her back to Illinois with them. Immediately after this visit, Mother rallied somewhat and spent less time bedridden, but soon learned that she was pregnant again. The birth of my parents' first son seemed to give my mother new purpose, but I remained "mother's helper." The only difference was that now I had to do all my other chores *and* help during the night with the baby. My parents had three other children after the first son, and they expected me to fill the role of "mother's helper" until I went to college. When Mother was in her eighties and she needed care-giving, one day she said to me, "In some ways you have taken care of me like a mother, even when you were a child." She also explained my success as an administrator of social welfare and educational programs when she said to my dean, "Betty should be good at that because she has always been bossy. She had to help me take care of her seven brothers and sisters."

I agree with my mother about my bossiness. To take charge or make a situation work for others such as siblings or members of my staff seems natural to me. Furthermore, whenever I am asked why I became a social worker, my reply is that I followed my mother's example of kindness. My mother would help strangers with the meager resources she had at her disposal. She even helped a White schoolmate who called me a nigger when she found out that he did not have shoes and suffered frostbite walking to our one-room school on frozen and rutted dirt roads. When I complained that her assistance was wasted on someone who had used such a terrible word, she said, "I don't care, no child should have to freeze in order to get to school." However, I have come to believe that my mother's kindness and respect for human life was only part of the reason for me to choose social work as a profession. I had an easily understood answer. I never attributed my choice of career to my desire to find out more about mental illness such as depression or paranoid schizophrenia, but surely that had to be part of the reason too.

Sometimes Mother's behavior was just unusual, cutting the telephone wires to prevent possible wiretaps, maybe even eccentric. I came to believe that it was more than that when she called me one evening during my junior year at University of Michigan with what seemed to be shocking news. "You know your father has raped your sisters. You can call the police or Reverend Stokes, and they will tell you that this happened on the way home from school last week." I was afraid for my sisters and seized with the desire to kill my father. Mother continued calmly, "Well, the girls won't tell you about this because they are afraid." I was stunned to silence and mumbled a goodbye. I went to my room and cried for the rest of the night. The next day, I was determined to find out the truth so I called Reverend Stokes, who had been my pastor for my entire life and whom I trusted completely. I haltingly repeated my mother's story. He told me that he had absolutely no knowledge of the situation and that he believed if it had happened, then it would have been made public.

Although I concluded from my conversation with Reverend Stokes that the dreadful things my mother said about my father were untrue, I went to the parking lot of Dad's job just as he came out of the huge industrial building and, with a mix of embarrassment and anger, repeated Mom's story to him. I watched to see if perhaps there were any signs of guilt; there were none. I was satisfied that my sisters were safe. I said, "If Mom continues to make such dangerous and unfounded allegations, then perhaps she should be institutionalized." Hanging his head in sadness, he said, "She will never do that again. I promise you. I do not want her to go away. I love her, and I will take care of it." Mom did continued to do eccentric things, but she never made any further sexual allegations to me about my father.

After this incident, I wanted to put a name to whatever possessed my mother to say such terrible things. I applied and was admitted to the University of Michigan's clinical social work program. My initial hope was that with professional training I could help others, especially teenagers, to solve their family problems.

In her middle and senior-citizen years, Mother's mental health moved like rain clouds over the landscape of her mind: Sometimes she was sunny and laughing, and the next moment a storm of paranoia and depression about her childhood seemed to overwhelm her. I learned to preempt the worst of the storms when I involved my mother in the fun parts of my life. For example, I forestalled storms when I gave my parents free tickets (donated by my sorority sisters) to the Michigan football games, scheduled shopping trips for my mother once I had a job, or invited her to attend a professional conference with me. One of my fondest memories is watching Mom try to appear unmoved by a very distinguished male African-American jazz vocalist from her youth, Arthur Prysock, as he leaned his immaculately-clad tall frame over to serenade her while we attended a conference in Cincinnati. After the song, he planted a kiss on Mom's cheek. The sun shone that evening.

Unlike my father, Mother never appeared too interested in the details of my professional or educational achievements. She mostly wanted to talk about my prospects for marriage and grandchildren although I told her, "Mother, I feel that I have already raised babies, and I am not in a hurry to do it again." Even so, I can still hear her saying during my early twenties, "You know that you are getting up there in age to find a husband. I had already had you when I was twenty-five." Then within months after I was married she started with, "When do you plan to have children?" followed by, "How is the pregnancy going? Can I take the baby, and care for him since you'll be working? When will you come to visit me with the baby? When will you have another baby?" Finally, when I was 60 years old, Mom said, "You are so good at raising children. I am proud of what you and Michael have done with Jahi and Aisha. Why don't you have another baby? You're not too old because I saw it on television – a woman older than you." At that point, I suggested to Mom that she ask one of her much younger daughters for another grandchild. She wouldn't stop with it so I said, "Mother, I had the inside of my uterus burned off in surgery; remember it caused me a lot of pain?" Her final mournful words on this topic: "Oh, there would be nowhere for the baby to hang onto. Well, I guess you won't be having one."

Hence, my solution to keep the lines of communication open with my parents from my undergraduate days forward was to let them guide the types of conversations that we had. I learned to speak to my mother about things that she was interested in such as children, cooking, movies, clothing, and the various doings of other family members. I tried to find activities we might both enjoy. On the other hand, I spoke to my father about my professional world, listened to his feedback about my research, and very reluctantly returned to the blueberry fields and barns when he wanted to show me the progress of his annual crops.

Seven Sisters and Brothers

"I only wanted two children," explained my mother when I asked her how she happened to have eight. It seems that the rhythm method of birth control (that relies on timing sexual intercourse with a woman's ovulation cycles) and condoms miserably failed Mom and Dad. An older male friend who himself had six children once told me that he had so many because he shot nothing but silver bullets. I asked what he thought about my dad's eight children and he replied, "Your Dad was shooting platinum!" So in my "sensitive" way, I later told my mom, "Well, you and Dad kind of overshot the number two."

On October 17, 2007, I gazed on Mom's body dressed in her favorite color, white, holding one of her favorite matching hats as she lay in the pink casket that we had chosen for her; her manicure and wig were lovely. Although I had dreaded seeing her prettied up by the undertakers' efforts, it turned out to be reassuring to see this unreal manufactured image that looked as she had at her very best. I also felt relief that she was no longer troubled by the terrible childhood memories of sexual abuse that had preoccupied many of her last days. Obviously, she no longer suffered the horrific and unremitting pain of the bladder cancer that virtually pinned her to the bed for most of her last year on earth. I was proud of the arrangements that I had coordinated with my siblings: the three red pots of chrysanthemums that symbolized the gift of life she had given my brothers while five white pots represented us girls; the large color-coordinated wreath with "Mother" on it; the soft melodious voice of her favorite religious artist, Mahalia Jackson, that drifted gently in the air; the special collage of her life that I prepared and called a "window to her world;" the service presided over by my sister Gail's pastor who had a doctorate of theology; the readings by a representative from each sibling's family; and especially the obituary with a few words from all of us, compiled by me and my sister, Frances. The obituary was really a ten-page biography that we illustrated with pictures of our family, Mom's greatest accomplishments; all of us had college degrees and many of her grandchildren had already finished theirs.

Sadly, this was the last time that all eight of us would be together. There would never be family holidays like the generation before us had, no reunions or visits that included all of my siblings, spouses, or their children, young people I had been close to since the day of their births.

A social worker explained to me that, "When a parent dies, sometimes family members will never speak to each other again. It is a reflection of long-simmering scores that were never settled before." Michael offered a different explanation, "Each of us grieves in a different way, and what you have seen with your siblings is how eight very different people handle their loss."

As I reflect on my family of origin, I realize that my parents always expected me to help my siblings and them. My father's first question to my future husband was, "When you all get married, can she still help her family?" Among the youngest of their respective families, my parents had been aided by their siblings and expected all of us to help each other, but they especially wanted me to do so as the oldest, to set an example. They urged me to give financial assistance, advice, or moral support. The down side of this is that, over the years, I grew to expect gratitude and respect, and I believe that some of my siblings grew to depend upon my assistance. These relationships had a bumpy road to travel. So after my mother died, I realized that for virtually my entire life (since age seven when Mom first got ill) I had taken on the role of "Big Betty," the bossy older sister, and I decided more than 50 years later that it was time to lay that burden down. Surprisingly, once I got out of the way, my siblings began to rely upon each other more; they began to look out for me, too.

Extended Family and the Doctoral Degree

By the middle of the 1950s, after our extended family became more accustomed to my parents' subsequent marriage after Dad's divorce, our home became a warm-weather destination for my grandmother and assorted uncles, aunts, cousins, and long-time friends who lived in Chicago, Texas, and, on rare occasions, California. Our family celebrations often resembled the movie "Soul Food," because good food was always the centerpiece for every gathering. My dad and uncles took charge of cooking the meat, usually grown on our farm, while my mother and aunts worked from late night into the early morning hours to cook delicious cakes, rolls, cornbread, salads, and other side dishes. Best of all was the homemade ice cream made with a custard cream poured into a device called a churn that was operated by hand, and thus only prepared on really special occasions. Although my mother had not learned how to cook as a child, my father taught her how because he had been a cook in the Navy. Eventually Mom's pastries rivaled Dad's in taste.

Cousins, Toni and Sherry LaRose, nearly the same age as Gail and me, were almost always present at these family gatherings where we ran races, rode bicycles, swapped stories about school, watched television when it rained, and played board or lawn games. All of us kids loved to eat; sometimes we would have contests. Once, Toni bested me when she ate six hot dogs to my five. We ate as we sat on the freshly-mown grass or at one of the lawn tables topped off by a huge pastel umbrella, a rummage sale gift from one of the relatives, or we may have been in the shade of the huge maple trees which fronted my parents' wide lawn. After the hot dogs, we ate the feast that our parents had prepared.

These are the best of my family recollections: the warmth of summer, the warmth of food, and the warmth of a large extended family.

I maintained contact with uncles, aunts, cousins, sisters, and brothers for most of the time that I was in the doctoral program. This contact was certainly not as often as I might have liked, and I missed many family occasions. One way that I kept these relationships intact occurred soon after I obtained a Master of Social Work. I was elected to the board of the National Association of Black Social Workers, and we traveled four times a year to various regions of the country for our meetings, regions where I visited family members. Later during the doctoral program, my job at the University of Chicago also required national travel; I made a point to stay with family whenever possible. I always purchased a large order of groceries on the University account as a thank-you gift when I stayed with family since the University made substantial savings because there was no cost for a hotel room. I believe this made me even more of a welcomed guest.

"They are not like trees, they are like spirits. The glens in which they grow are not like places, they are like haunts – haunts of the . . . gods," an author once observed about redwood trees (Masefield as cited in Rasp, 1999, p. 52). This feeling of a positive yet eternal spirit came to me during a hike in the California Redwood forest, then guided me on a gentle reverie of the many visits I had made to my Aunt Johnnie who had lived in nearby Palo Alto, California. This last visit to commemorate her life was one in a long series that stretched back over more than three decades of business travel that had brought me to the San Francisco/Palo Alto area and into contact with my mother's older sister, an aunt that I had seen in person perhaps two or three times during childhood. My parents had both emphasized the importance of maintaining family ties: "You need to see your grandma, aunt, uncle, or cousin (whoever might live in the city I planned to visit)," they directed. My dad's example included routine visits to Illinois, especially for holidays, where most of his siblings and mother lived (about a three-hour drive from rural South Haven) while my mother maintained contact with far-distant relatives such as her sister, Johnnie, through letters, telephone calls, holiday cards, and rare trips, mostly for funerals.

Initially, I began my visits to Aunt Johnnie because I was a dutiful daughter doing my mother's bidding when she knew I was going to California for business. I made my first trip to the San Francisco Bay area when I was in my mid-twenties. I had never been to California and only remembered seeing sun, bikini swim suits, movie stars, and palm trees on television, so I believed that this first visit/business trip was a great chance to have fun in an exotic tropical locale. This is the reason that in 1976 I stepped off the airplane wearing high-heeled sandals, white summer-weight slacks, and a bright red halter top which just covered the absolute bare essentials. I was met by a blast of cold air that felt as though it had escaped from a polar ice cap. My aunt, looking like a twin to my mother who spoke in virtually the same Texas sing-song drawl, exclaimed, "Get this child a coat!"

As I shivered on the way to their car, I said, "I thought everyone in California wore bathing suits?"

My aunt and her daughters, my cousins, had big belly laughs about this, and my aunt explained, "Honey, you are in northern California, and it is almost always cool here. Whenever it reaches over 80—which it doesn't very often—then we all celebrate. Tonight when Lois takes you to Fisherman's Wharf, the temperature will be in the 40s." I still found this difficult to believe, but sure enough, when Cousin Lois took me out to dinner I was very comfortable bundled in my borrowed *faux fur* coat.

Lois really knocked herself out to show me a good time. While we ate dinner at a diner on the Wharf, we saw a very short and handsome Black man dressed in a white shirt and tight blue jeans; I recognized the famous composer and conductor, Quincy Jones, with his then-wife actress Peggy Lipton, a television star. I remember thinking that in her private life the tall and thin Ms. Lipton appeared quite pale and very plain-looking and not at all as attractive as her television character. After dinner Lois insisted that I see every inch of the Wharf followed by a tour of the San Francisco art galleries where people apparently paid astounding sums, equivalent to a year of my salary, for abstract art that just looked like a mishmash of colors to me. Naturally, Lois had to show me the more risqué clubs where women and men entertained in clothes even skimpier than mine. My Midwestern mind whirled as we had a drink and someone dressed only in cow udders and a bell—I could not focus on the rest of the body to determine what was in the nether regions— entertained.

For many years, I continued to have great fun with Aunt Johnnie's clan. In 1978, when I was pregnant with Jahi, I took Michael to meet my California relatives. During the two days we visited we had a marvelous time, minus the risqué clubs, saw the sights, and ate huge meals because my aunt insisted that I was eating for two; I think that she fed me for three. There were the lumberjack breakfasts, followed by lunch in an artists' colony across the Golden Gate Bridge and then a barbeque where at least 20 of my cousins gathered to meet us. We had steaks, sausage, ribs, chicken, salads, cakes, pies, cookies, punch, pop, cocktails, milk, and more. I could hardly sleep at night because there was just not enough room to hold the baby and digest the food too. Before Michael and I left California, my cousin Pam and I compared baby bumps to see who was bigger and surprisingly, even though we were about the same number of months pregnant, I lost the competition.

Almost 30 years later, when I sensed that my Aunt Johnnie neared the end of her life, I used my by-now standard operating procedure to couple business with family visits, and I attended a national conference in San Francisco. I took the opportunity to find out more about the person rather than the hostess who had entertained me so often.

She said, "I was four years old when my father died . . . and I went to the eighth grade (meaning she was probably fourteen years old) and then stayed home to care for my mother who was sick a long time and for my younger sister and brother." Aunt Johnnie elaborated on her youth in segregated Texas during the early 1900s where "We had to walk five miles to school . . . . Sometimes we had to get up and leave in the dark. The White School was closer to us and they had a bus, but we were not allowed to attend that school." She also told me that after the death of her mother, she married at age seventeen, in large part to escape a sexually abusive stepfather.

The fact that Aunt Johnnie did not have much formal education amazed me because I had always seen her as quite cultured in manner and fashionably dressed. On the very rare occasions that she visited us in Michigan, traveling from California, she and her daughters looked like beautiful models to me. During this conversation I realized that from an early age I have always equated beautiful clothing and correct diction with education.

Throughout the years my aunt had only one complaint about our relationship: that I should always visit when in California.

Once I made the mistake of calling her instead of visiting when I was on vacation nearby. She exclaimed with evident sobs in her voice, "I am crying—to know that you are so close and cannot stop by just to say hello to your family." In retrospect, I believe that we generally got along well due in large measure to my willingness to be adored. Aunt Johnnie's love for her kin and joy in getting firsthand news of her sister and other relatives in the Midwest was boundless. She told me that she believed that she had been quite important in my life.

At her funeral, I said:

> I am Dr. Betty Brown-Chappell and Johnnie Reed was my aunt. My mother was her sister and my family lived in Michigan, which is a long way from California. My parents raised eight children and all of us have received a college education. It was only last year that I learned that my Aunt Johnnie had not been able to finish high school because she took care of her sick mother, then at seventeen when her mother died, she took the responsibility to care for her younger brother and sister, my mother. Think about it—at seventeen she was only a child herself. What were you doing at seventeen? I certainly would not have had the ability to care for two other children. I attribute the educational success of my family to Johnnie Reed. Thank you, Aunt Johnnie.

The next day as I walked among the redwoods near San Francisco after my brief eulogy, I began to see Aunt Johnnie's life as I did the giant trees, a symbol of continuity and strength, as they are in some Native-American cultures. Like Aunt Johnnie, they at once represent the past and future because these giants seem never to die, rather one may tumble to the ground because of a lightning strike or the tremendous weight of hundreds of branches which reportedly support animals unique to the environment living in redwood meadows formed high, high in the sky[5]. Just as my family in Michigan had been separated since my birth by the continental United States from Aunt Johnnie's family in California, the tree-top meadows of the redwoods thrive, as did my family, because of the tree's root system (Aunt Johnnie as maternal matron), genetically linked but existing with no recognition of the other. When this amazing tree-world within itself topples, then it will yield sprouts and the tree literally rises again, the genetic composition never changing; one might say the tree is eternal. My mind dwelled upon the significance of the debt that all the branches of our "family tree" owed Aunt Johnnie, who had taken on the burden to raise her younger brother and sister, my fourteen-year-old mother, and had thus spawned a myriad of fruitful lives to come.[6]

Another extended family member taught me not to take myself too seriously. I visited my Uncle Roosevelt Hawkins shortly after I graduated from the University of Chicago; he lived in nearby Evanston. After military service in Korea, Uncle Hawkins moved north from Louisiana and met a lovely woman, my father's sister, Goldie Brown, who was several years his senior. My uncle was quite a character in looks and actions; he had an unusual reddish-brown complexion with hair to match; he had done manual labor all his life and now seated in his kitchen was in his seventies but still seemed strong enough to "turn a windmill with a crank." A widower for some years by 1992, he sat in his favorite chair as he looked out on the quiet street where he had lived for decades and where he now presided over dirty dishes and piles of cigarette butts on his

---

[5] The tallest such tree is reported as 379 feet, which is higher than a 35-story building (http://www.nps.gov/redw/faqs.htm).

[6] After she moved to Waco, TX, the neighbors, Dr. and Mrs. Adams, helped Aunt Johnnie and her husband care for her two younger siblings by giving them food and clothing. Eventually, the Adams took care of my mother on a full-time basis.

dining table. He squinted through the ever-present smoke and said, "Well, I heard you finished that degree you been working on for so long." To which I responded, "Yeah, I am doctor now, but don't ask for no prescriptions 'cause I can't heal anything." Uncle Hawkins' lips peeled back over his large teeth, and he threw his head back and forth as he had one of the biggest belly laughs I have ever witnessed. We both continued to chuckle about this line for hours after; my uncle would repeat part of the line, and we'd be off again to laugh harder than the first time I said it. Uncle Hawkins even repeated the story to other family members, and it became one of my standard lines to ease family tensions over the differences in our education.

During the seven years that it took me to complete the doctoral degree, I missed many family ceremonies, such as my sister's second wedding or a funeral for my husband's stepmother. I had to dash from my father's side immediately after his surgery for colon cancer. When it was all over and I graduated with the doctorate, then I tried to make up for these lapses by being present even before I was asked. For example, soon after my dissertation hearing, I took my children for a week-long trip to see their grandparents in South Haven where we made ourselves helpful. Since then I have made it a habit to be present to provide help and support when there is a serious illness or death in the family. I am often the first one to help out with homemade baked goods, roasts, or soup.

My dear advisor during my doctoral studies, Dr. Dolores Norton (Norton et al., 1978), has an early theory about African Americans—one could substitute the word first-generation here—and how we cope with the larger society and within our own culture. She suggests that we must live in both worlds and learn customs of behavior for both; there may be different figures of speech, pronunciation, clothing styles, politics, hobbies, and so on. While it may be a burden on middle-class and upwardly mobile folks to deal with this "twoness," I have found it a reality of my existence that I am content with. I am not alone.

References

Norton, D. et al. (1978). *Inclusion of ethnic minority content in social work curriculum.* New York, NY: Council on Social Work Education.

Rasp, R. A. (1999). *Redwood: The story behind the scenery.* Wickenberg, AZ: KC Publications, INC.

Riley, R. (2004, January 25). Sexy is as sexy does. *Detroit Free Press*, pp. H1-2.

Study Questions

1. What are your greatest fears when you think about higher education?
2. How do they compare to the ones that I describe in this chapter?
3. Have you encountered family resistance or lack of understanding about your plans to complete a degree?
4. I examined my role in my birth family. What is yours? How might it relate to your desire to obtain an advanced degree?
5. Discuss why it may have been important for me to nominate my husband as "Sexiest Man Alive."
6. In what ways do you anticipate maintaining your romantic relationship with a partner, lover, better half, husband or wife?
7. How do you expect to achieve humility yet take pride in your educational achievements?

Photo Album

My parents Benjamin
Franklin Brown and Clara
Lucille Williams as young
adults circa mid 1940s.

Clara Lucille Brown holds
the infant Betty in 1946.

Farm life in southwest
Michigan- early 1950s.

Lower left corner – Betty Brown circa 1953.

L-R Benjamin, Clara Lucille, Sandra, Betty, Gail, Frances (back row) Brown enjoy family time. In front are Benjamin, Jr., Daniel, Carolyn, and David Brown shown at a picnic in Evanston, IL.

Members of the Student Senate at South Haven, Michigan High School gathered for annual photo in 1964. Betty's first elected office. Betty is in the back row, far right. Photo by Appleyard Photography, South Haven, Michigan.

Pledges of Nu Chapter – Delta Sigma Theta Sorority – spring 1966 at U of Michigan. Betty is seated center.

Thanksgiving Day circa 1985 - Clara Lucille, Benjamin Brown, and their children in their rural South Haven, Michigan home.

Betty Brown and Michael Chappell share a tender moment in 1975, the year they married.

Michael Jahi Chappell at birth November 1, 1978, is cuddled by his mother, Betty Brown-Chappell.

February 17, 1982 heralds the birth of Aisha Ebony Chappell.

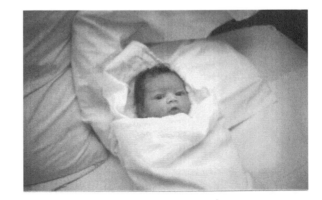

Detroit's Cass Corridor Safety for Senior Citizens open house circa 1975. Betty Brown's first professional grant.

Betty Brown-Chappell, President, National Association of Social Workers - Michigan Chapter, chairs meeting circa 2005.

Betty Brown-Chappell receives her doctoral degree, 1991.

Professor Pastora San Juan Cafferty, chairperson of Betty Brown-Chappell's dissertation committee.

Clockwise from upper left:

Best friend Sheila Malone and Betty Brown-Chappell.

Betty Brown-Chappell and Detroit City Council President Mary Ann Mahaffey, mentor.

U of C Professor Dolores "Dodie" Norton, mentor, and Betty Brown-Chappell.

Chapter 5 — Isms:
Classism, Racism, and Sexism

Five hundred people rose to their feet to give me the first standing ovation of my life. I heard the sound of their collective movement before I realized what was happening. I had yet to say a word! My tall and distinguished husband of more than 36 years extended his warm hand to welcome me on the stage; he had just given me a wonderful introduction—calling me a drum major for justice in keeping with Dr. King's approach to advocacy. I was applauded because I had won my university's Martin Luther King Humanitarian Award for 2012. My speech on January 16, 2012, best reflects how I feel about no longer being poor—not low-income, but po' as we sometimes say in the Black community.

As the applause went on, I opened my arms to symbolically embrace the crowd; then I applauded them and said,

> First and foremost I want to recognize my parents, Benjamin Franklin and Lucille Brown, who are not alive today to celebrate this award but whose love for me and my seven brothers and sisters still endures.
>
> It is important to me in the context of our contentious public discourse about the nature of work, poverty, and poor people to say that I come from a very humble—yes,

poor—background. I know my husband will tell you that it was almost yesterday that we were poor in our marriage. My father could only attend school through the 7th grade because he had to go to work at 14; my mother was an orphan who despite this obstacle became a high school graduate. Both of my parents were part of the 99% of people who work virtually every day of their lives to eke out an existence—my father was an auto worker and my mom was quite busy making a home for her 8 children—everyone of whom graduated from college. My admiration for my parents means that I will not join the discourse to denigrate and vilify poor folks. For most of my life I have been in the ranks of the poor and near-poor . . . I will not bash affirmative action because I have lived it . . . I will not disparage teachers because I am one . . .

This is where I join the discussion about poverty: "**If you are not part of the solution, you are part of the problem.**" Part of the problem that I have observed on this campus is the lack of scholarship assistance for talented low-income students. This is why my children, my husband, and I have endowed the Brown-Chappell scholarship, which will be available for students as long as there is an Eastern Michigan University. We donated these funds because the people we admire are not (amazingly) Donald Trump and his ilk, but rather the Eastern Michigan University students who enter college on a wing and a prayer as I did, and who struggle against mighty odds in our cut-back society to excel.

My family has only one scholarship to give each year, but we hope that there may be many others here today who will join with us to make similar scholarship contributions.

I am not the sole recipient of this prestigious award: There is a legion of individuals to whom this belongs. I want to introduce those in the room who have brought me to this moment in time. They have counseled me wisely, argued the merits of policy, served with me on innumerable committees, helped me on projects, laughed with me, and loved me without reservation:

You have already met my husband, Michael. Our daughter, Ms. Aisha Ebony Chappell, is a program director in the NYC public schools and a geometry teacher. Her brother, Dr. Jahi Chappell, is a professor of Earth and Environmental Science and Justice at Washington State University.

I also want to recognize my brothers: Ben and David and David's wife, Deb. My sisters Gail, Frances, and Carolyn are here, and Carolyn's daughters, Maia and Riana. Can all my family members please stand?

I especially want to give heart-felt thanks to my nominators, Dr. Laura Davis, Prof. Bonnie Miller, Dr. Crystal Mills, Ms. LaNesha Debardeladen, and Dr. Ann Alvarez. Finally, thank you to all of the faculty, staff, McNair alumni, and students in the School of Social Work, and both the College of Health and Human Services and the Honors College, who have helped me as I strived to be a "drum major for justice" in Dr. Martin Luther King's activist spirit, and as Lanie Guinier (the keynote speaker and first African-American woman tenured at Harvard Law School) reminded us: We are part of a collective community of caring.

You have taught me so much during my 16-year journey at EMU. I am deeply grateful. Thank you. I am honored to receive the MLK 2012 Humanitarian Award on behalf of my family, friends, colleagues, and students.

It has been a very long road from the poverty of rural southern Michigan to my present blessed life.

Despite this late-life award that I received, I still find that I experience some subtle covert discrimination in my professional world as a tenured full professor. For example, I find on occasion that my remarks are not acknowledged during meetings when perhaps my blackness, femaleness, and now advanced age render me voiceless and invisible to others. In 2010, I convened a panel of two other female colleagues and we discussed, among other topics, the subject of professional invisibility with young women in our state. Each panelist recalled instances during professional meetings[7] when we advanced an idea but no one in the room, including other women or people of color, acknowledged our comments. At such times everyone else seemed to have a sudden urge to look at their shoes, out the window, at their fingernails, at one another. They look for any place aside from the woman of color who has just spoken. A moment passes while folks wait to hear from someone who is more respected, perhaps not a woman, a first-generation scholar, or an African American. Frequently, a man—Black or White—will repeat the same comment that we have made, but now the group finds the idea acceptable and discusses it with relish.

My co-presenters, a Latina and an African American, and I solved the "ism" problems by working harder than others, making strategic choices about when to confront such behavior, and realizing that ultimately it doesn't matter who is credited for a solution or idea in discussions, as long as the idea is adopted. We all have developed "thick skin" about workplace slights despite the many prestigious degrees, titles, promotions, or size of our paycheck.

We may have a piece of the American Dream, but one of my White male mentors told me, "Well don't take any of this too seriously because we also treat each other like shit." He wanted me to know that there are few if any persons in the work force who are accepted by other colleagues solely on merit. Folks in

[7] This is similar to a situation FDIC Chairwoman Blair experienced and described in a *New York Times Magazine* article (Nocera, 2011) where, "Men controlled the narrative" in her work.

the dominant culture find faults with each other that are not based on "isms." In the work place, the person who finds fault, criticizes, or makes light of fellow workers strives to be dominant, like a playground bully. "If I bully you first, then I take charge of a situation or gain more respect." (Abraham Lincoln was constantly derided by "friends" and foes alike.) I have heard White men say behind each other's backs, "He may have been on television yesterday (got a promotion, published a book, obtained a grant or fellowship), but he is really not too bright— that stuff really doesn't count." For those of us who are minority, first-generation, and poor, we have the added burden that past poverty can be a present obstacle; being a woman can remain an obstacle; and having brown skin or speaking Spanish may continue to be an obstacle. We should also add membership in the gay, lesbian, and transgendered community to the list of outsiders in academia and the workplace.

Classism is society's preference for those in the middle and upper classes, demonstrated through individual and institutional responses. Many in our society, individually or collectively, are more likely to assign positive characteristics to someone who has the money to buy an expensive automobile or fur coat while looking unfavorably on someone who drives a beater and wears threadbare clothing. Institutionally, it will be a rare person of the lower class who will be able to gain admission to an Ivy League institution of higher education such as Harvard University or other upper tier universities. Our poverty throws up barriers that will probably mean we cannot pay the tuition and fees which for a 2012 Harvard student were $54,496 (personal expenses and travel not included); we probably did not attend a private preparatory high school that is highly respected by the admissions committee. Very few of us scored as well as the higher income high school senior on the standardized admissions tests because we did not realize we needed to study for it, or that there is a method taught to higher income/class students by teachers, parents, and tutors that will likely yield a score high enough to obtain Harvard's admission. Finally, we are not "legacy" admits. A "legacy" is a student whose parents are graduates and who will get preferential treatment in the form of extra points on the admissions rating.

Classism and Poverty Up Close and Personal

Poverty is when you don't own the boots to pull yourself up.

Being poor is also going to your first day on the job at the City County Building in Detroit, proud of your newly-earned Master of Social Work degree, mingling with the sharply dressed workforce that rush to and fro, but making sure that your feet stay flat on the floor to hide the holes in the soles of your shoes.

On a hot sticky day in 1971, I parked my car across from the Building and reported for an interview with the director of the Bureau of Drug Abuse, a brute of a man who was a former police officer with the crew-cut blond hair to prove he had been a cop. I really hoped that I would get the job despite the fact that I knew absolutely nothing about drug abuse or program administration, which would be the focus of the position. What I did know was that I was desperate for work: I was two months behind in my rent, and rice and beans were all I could afford for every meal of the day. I asked my parents for help, but Dad had been off work and without a paycheck for over a week. With several remaining children in the home, I knew he really could not help me. I could not think of anyone else to ask for help. When I parked my car, I had less than two dollars in my purse, enough money to pay for the expected hour-long interview.

The director immediately offered me the job and asked if I could stay for the rest of the day on payroll. I gulped, "Yes, I can stay." I was afraid that if I hesitated, someone else might get the job instead of me. The closer I got to the end of that first day on the job, the more I pressed my feet to the ground—trying to stop time—to put off the inevitable moment when I would have to face the insurmountable problem of how to get my car out of the parking lot with the little money in my purse, when I knew that the cost for the entire day's parking was $5.00, more than twice what I had with me.

Promptly at 4:30 p.m., the offices around me began to empty out of the confident and fashionable occupants. Their glossy shoes seemed to improbably glide across the drab office floor. Those shoes matched the other workers' business clothes but did not resemble my now-sweaty and bedraggled ones. At the end of this day, everyone else seemed to be crisp and confident. Yet I stood stock still pushing my feet into the vinyl tile of my eleventh-floor cubby hole of an office and hoped for a miracle as I gazed down at the lot across the street where I knew my car was parked. I shared the office with an older Black man named "David Poe." David cleared his throat and said gently in his resonant bass voice, "Honey, do you need any money for parking?" I turned and looked upon his thin honey-colored face where I saw kindness in pale green eyes. I accepted David's loan of five dollars. I accepted a free lunch every Friday, and I accepted the $500 that he and another male colleague, "Stephen Jones," offered to me when it took three successive payroll periods before I received my first check.

Sitting with my new colleagues at a very exclusive restaurant in the Ponchatrain Hotel—a setting populated by music and sports celebrities, union officials, politicians, and high-ranking civil servants—I found out the reason for my new colleagues' extraordinary kindness and generosity. David explained as Stephen, a short chocolate-colored Black man in his fifties, nodded repeatedly in agreement, "Betty, we have both worked for the City of Detroit for over thirty-five years. Our children have finished college. We are quite comfortable financially. You are just starting out, and you aren't being paid on time; this is not right. But it happens; it is not your fault. Our money will probably mean a lot to you in setting up your new apartment, but if you *never* pay us back we will be all right. All you have to do is enjoy this lunch. Order anything that you want; I am having sirloin steak. When we leave here, the three of us will go to the bank, and you will tell us how much money you need. We can probably cover any amount between us so don't hesitate. We don't want to even discuss repayment right now. It is a pleasure to help you get your life started."

Almost in tears, I stared first at the crisply starched white table cloth, then looked down at the gleaming china plate that now held an expensive sirloin steak which my two benefactors had urged me to order. I was very humbled, and very grateful. I gulped down some water, and considered my desperate financial situation. My friends had already helped me out as much as they could. I reasoned that I had to accept the kindness of strangers to pay all my overdue bills, to cover moving costs from Ann Arbor to Detroit, and to guarantee that I could get to work in the coming weeks until a paycheck finally arrived. I did not see any other way. Ultimately, these two men kept their word; they never asked for repayment and continued to support me at work as I learned to administer and evaluate drug abuse clinics, a job that my concentration in group and individual social work had not really prepared me to do. I did pay them back monetarily. I also paid them every time I helped one of my friends or family members who found themselves in similar situations. This experience reinforced the generosity of spirit that my parents had so often emphasized during my childhood, and it made me even more dedicated both professionally and personally to alleviate poverty. At the time, I felt that I had traveled a very long distance from a working-class existence in rural South Haven, Michigan, to the fancy Ponchatrain Hotel restaurant.

Although most people in the twenty-first century are very familiar with the word and concept of "*poverty*," it was not a concept or word that I understood very well during my upbringing. Unlike current times when television commentators occasionally do specials on the topic, it was not discussed on television in my childhood because we did not even have routine electrical service (storms often blew our electrical wires down and we resorted to using candles and kerosene lamps) until I was about eight, and television was not available coast to coast until 1951. My father purchased one of the first televisions in our neighborhood during the mid 1950s, and our family used to host the neighbors on Friday nights to watch the vague shadows of boxers and referees on a twelve-inch monitor that also blasted out the sounds of crowds cheering so shrilly that I left the room and joined my sisters to play with our dolls. Instead of social commentary, television was dominated by comedy and variety shows starring mostly well-dressed White people who joked about all of their problems: drinking too much (*Red Skelton Show* or *Jackie Gleason*), marital arguments (*I Love Lucy*), or squabbles with the kids (*Father Knows Best*). Unlike my childhood experiences, television problems did not involve hunger, dental pain, lack of medical care, or too little money for too many family members. Also, in contrast to today's twenty-four-hour news cycle where reporting on poverty has been in and out of vogue more times than I can count, we were not treated to a regular diet of murder, national disasters, or war on CNN or Headline News. Rather the fifties news programs my family watched from our overstuffed used couch in rural southwestern Michigan might last for fifteen to thirty minutes and flash images of the hydrogen bomb, the president of the United States, stock market reports, or on rare occasion high crimes of treason or murder. Television was coupled with a few celebrity-focused magazines to provide a glimpse into a White world inhabited by funny or dramatic people with beautiful clothes and teeth, who were not hungry, Black, or farmers like we were. In many ways our experience of the outside world was so limited that it effectively placed us children in a protected bubble.

Thus, I *never* recall news about the poor or poverty with the exception of a few lines I overheard candidate and future President John F. Kennedy utter in his 1960 presidential campaign. When a wealthy, handsome, and educated man like Kennedy "discovered" poverty and showed compassion for poor persons from Appalachia (White and deserving of assistance) in his discussion, other Americans also began to pay attention to the issue of poverty. As a teenager and young adult I witnessed President Johnson's attempt to keep the social order with national policies like equal opportunity in education and affirmative action in employment; as an adult I, along with many other people of color, would benefit from such policies. However, decades after my childhood when non-violent protests for economic and social justice were followed by race riots in Watts, Detroit, Chicago, and other major cities, the pendulum swung away from anti-poverty laws, and politicians specifically identified much of the African-American population as undeserving poor.[8]

These events did not impact my 1950s existence as an African-American child; I knew that my family sometimes had too little money, scarce food, and medical or dental care, but it was just the "normal" condition of my life. Plus, there were only one or two families in our community who weren't in the same boat.

The most memorable instance of poverty was the sacrifice of my piggy bank to purchase food. My uncle Herbert Brown gave me a white piggy bank with big red cheeks as a present. This glass pig was at least as big as a gallon jar, and I faithfully fed the pig the coins that numerous aunts, uncles, and adult cousins gave me. I also added a portion of my earnings from picking berries in the summer. One day, after saving for at least a couple of years, I came into our dining room where I kept the pig; it had been shattered into pieces. I cried out, "What happened to my pig?"

---

[8] I discuss at length in my dissertation (1991), *The Black Movement Model of Mayoral Leadership,* the historical events and trends which led to African American poor becoming a proxy for all poor. Once this proxy was established by President Ronald Reagan (1981-89) and a series of social authors, I argue that the intellectual foundation was laid for the political wherewithal to pass policies which significantly decreased redistributive allocations to the poor.

Soon my loud moans, screams, and tears drew my father into the room and he said sternly, "Betty, there is no choice if you and your sisters want to eat and have electricity in our house. I do not have enough money to buy food and pay the electrical bill because we are off work for a while." His factory was on automobile change-over to retool for the next year's model, I learned, and workers were not paid during this procedure. Gripped by this adult situation, I stared fixedly at the back of the pig, bashed into chalky pieces with a hammer. I don't remember clearly all the details of that day, but I do know that I agreed that we had to have food and electricity for our family, and I do remember that I thought we needed money. I just did not know that this was poverty.

"Frank, I don't have anything for dinner tonight," said my mother in a matter-of-fact tone of voice, perhaps not to alarm us kids. As she stood looking into the refrigerator in her thin housedress, she explained why Dad, already tired from eight hours of manual labor pouring molten aluminum, had to go to the woods beyond our house and hunt for game immediately. "We already ate that old hen you killed last night. Remember we had it with some dumplings? It's gone now because the children ate the rest for lunch." We kids only knew that the chewy chicken and plump dumplings our mother made were mighty tasty, hot, and filling. Sometimes dinner might be a little late because it might take Dad past our usual dinner time to track and kill an animal. It had to be skinned or plucked, then gutted. Most often he brought home rabbits, and they always tasted good the way my mother cooked them with onions from the garden and smothered in heavy brown gravy, and we were glad to have it. Waiting until Dad finished hunting for food or killed an old hen in the hen house for dinner was normal for us.

My first big hint that our existence could be called *poverty* occurred one day after school when I asked my mother if we could donate some food to the poor because the teacher was taking up a special collection for Christmas. My mother chuckled

95

and said, "Honey, we are the poor. They are likely to give some of that food to us." Well, I begged for something to take, and my mother finally gave me a can of Spam to take to school. We all really hated that salty fat pink stuff which had been given to us by Uncle Harry, and it stayed around our house until dust collected on the top of it. So it turned out that on the day of the food drive I didn't feel so different from the other kids for two reasons. First, there were only a couple whose family made donations and second, I suspected that my classmates knew I brought the dusted-off Spam because our family really didn't like it.

It was not uncommon for kids in my one-room school to be absent because of a toothache, and many of their gum lines were green or dark yellow because they probably did not own toothpaste or a brush. Sometimes Gerald, a blond boy in my grade whose family had not returned to Alabama after the fall crops had been harvested, came to school with his jaw twice its normal size. He was in so much pain that he could not concentrate to read the lessons and had to sit in the back of the school with his head down. In contrast, my toothaches were relieved by oil of cloves, and my cavities never interfered with school. So I felt lucky that when the nerves in my teeth sounded the pain alarm, my parents knew how to dip a tiny piece of sterile cotton in oil of cloves and then gently apply it to the hole in my teeth. This ritual continued until my parents took me on three or four occasions to the dentist to have the rotten teeth removed. I was afraid, but I welcomed the coming relief from pain. After all, my father had all his teeth removed when I was a young child, and my mother had had several removed soon after birthing her fourth child. Lucky for me that the anesthesia held, because I remember once my dentist used what looked like a small hammer and braced himself against the chair to extract my teeth; apparently I have very stubborn roots. In my drug stupor, I felt concern for the poor dentist who finished the extraction and collapsed his chubby body into a chair as he wiped his brow from all the physical labor of separating me from my rotten teeth.

The practice of dental cleaning, fluoridated water, and toothpaste did not reach our rural community until I became an adolescent. I was relieved after my teeth were pulled because the absence of large cavities meant that I no longer had to avoid chewing on the sides of my mouth. As a result I had a wonderful sense of freedom when I visited a friend or relatives' home and sat down to share a meal.

Even so, since I started to work during my first year of college I have never let my cavities or dental hygiene go untended. I got timely fillings for cavities and then learned to brush my teeth properly (at age 35); I learned eventually to floss, and I get my teeth cleaned twice a year. Yet poverty rises with me each day of what has become a very fortunate life. It is in my mouth in the morning when I run my tongue over the gold, silver, and porcelain fillings in every one of the teeth that are left in my head. I feel lucky to have those expensive fillings; I feel lucky that there are only a few teeth still missing and that only my dentist can see the empty spaces which would otherwise announce my earlier poverty to the world. I feel lucky that I have an employer-sponsored dental insurance plan and can maintain my general health and present to the world a bright "Colgate" smile. I feel lucky that I could afford braces in my thirties so that my teeth now give the illusion of being straight. I feel lucky that my gums were cut away from the bone to cure the gum disease that ultimately killed my maternal grandmother in her forties and left my mother and her siblings as orphans. They suffered life-long heartache from her loss. I know that my parents would have been spared the enormous amount of pain from tooth extraction and ill-fitted false teeth had they been able to afford better dental care.

Thus, my path from poverty to the PhD degree has led me to believe that every person in our country should have dental health care. No one should die, as my maternal grandmother did, or have their gums cut away or their teeth all removed because they are too poor to afford dental care.

In addition to dental care, I also treasure indoor plumbing and, even given environmental concerns, lots of hot water for baths and showers. Although the precise dates are lost to the decades separating me from my early childhood, I do remember that when my family first moved to rural Michigan, we did not have indoor plumbing for several years. This meant that I, my parents, and my little sisters either had to eliminate our bodily wastes in a metal pot or we went to an outhouse located a short distance behind the main house. I remember that I did not like the outhouse because it was sometimes cold, especially in the fall and winter early mornings, and sometimes it had varmints like mice, rats, snakes, spiders, or mosquitoes in it or near it. Also, my father was always on the lookout for hawks that might swoop down to capture one of our few chickens for their dinner. Dad sometimes kept his shotgun in the outhouse so he could step out and kill one of the hawks who preyed on our chickens. The land where our house stood had recently been woodland, so the varmints did not know that the outhouse was off limits. As a young child I was frightened by the gun because it summoned a bloody end to life, death, that I spied by peeking at the lifeless corpses of the dead varmints.

My parents never let us go to the outhouse alone. It was a big achievement when my father added a second stool to the outhouse because it meant that we did not have to wait our turn. My parents took great pride in keeping the outhouse smelling clean. Meanwhile, if both seats were occupied, we had to use that "old pot" as my sister Gail used to say. I recall sometimes waking up to the uric acid smell of the "old pot" even though it had a lid; I was glad when my parents emptied it every morning but hated it when I was sometimes asked to do it. It was a stinky job.

Without indoor plumbing, we took baths only on the weekends when my father could help pour the huge pots of hot water that were boiled on the stove into our big gray tin tub.

Initially, Gail and I bathed together in the tub, and that was all right. But things began to get a little more crowded when Frances had to bathe with us. When the fourth baby came along, Mom bathed her in the big dark blue and white speckled canning pot, but finally the baby was too big to fit into the pot. This is when Mom figured out that she would have us bathe in shifts, and the last shift had to sit in the soap scum that rose to the top of the tub after the first two sisters were clean. I always hurried to either get in the first shift or washed quickly standing up during the second shift to avoid as much scum as possible. In between weekly baths we took what were known as "spit" baths when warmed water from the tea kettle was placed in a washing bowl and you wiped off the most important areas with a washcloth. Again, I did not feel deprived because it was obvious from the body odors that filled our small schoolroom that many of my classmates did not take baths as often as I did. Some smelled of old urine, others of that special super strong sweat that goes with puberty—almost as strong as a skunk smell but with a little extra musk. Other kids had manure that had ripened on the bottom of their shoes from doing daily chores in the cow pens. Last, there were some that had really oily smells rising up from hair that hadn't been washed for quite a while and might be decorated with head lice.

We got plumbing in the house with running hot water when my parents paid off the mortgage and could devote "discretionary" money to it; I think I must have been about ten at the time.

During my early childhood, my family paid for medical care if one of us (1) was unconscious, (2) had profuse bleeding, (3) had extreme trouble breathing, or (4) obviously had a communicable disease such as measles or mumps. They paid for Mother to have prenatal and delivery care. Practically speaking this meant that there was no care for third degree burns, cuts of any size, dislocations, rashes, or sprains. My parents learned from an older neighbor, a transplant from Louisiana, to use special home remedies such as a goose grease and onion poultice that they applied to the chest of anyone who had a persistent cough; in the winter they gave us cod liver or castor oil and orange juice to make sure that we did not get constipated and that we had vitamins.

As I recounted earlier, as kids we were frequently clothed through a combination of hand-me-downs from relatives and clothes we bought with summer earnings. However, clothing was one area where our parents had long-standing disagreements. Dad, who as youth had won a best-dressed contest, had only two dress suits, a brown one and a gray plaid one until I turned 18 when he bought a Johnny Carson suit for my graduation.

From early childhood until I left home, it seemed that Mom and Dad argued heatedly and repeatedly about Mom's desire for new dress clothes for herself and us children. She sometimes purchased *Vogue* magazine and looked in the Sunday news supplements or the Sears' catalog for the "ideal" outfit. At these times, my sisters and I would gather around Mom and ask, "Mom, which outfit do you really like?" She would point out one or two and we would promise, "Mom, don't worry when we get big and have money, then we will buy that outfit." Decades later we kept that promise. Unlike Mom, who believed that it was always essential to "put up a good front," our father said repeatedly, "Why do I need to put good money into a new suit when all I do is farm and work in the factory? The two suits I have are good enough for the rare occasions I have to go to church, and I can rent a tuxedo if we go to a formal dance."

Despite the inconvenience of the outhouse, lack of dental or medical care, or my parents' bickering about clothing, I had almost reached puberty before I realized that our family was considered poor by the outside world.

Poverty is a Family Secret

I was a nosey child; nowadays they call it "precocious." Being nosey meant that I found out things that adults didn't want me to know or see.

It was during the late 1950s and I would have been about twelve. Aunt Frankie's high-pitched voice rang out in the dawn stillness of her home in Evanston, Illinois. "I don't see why they keep having all those children. Enough is enough! They're so poor that they can hardly provide for the five they already have; now Lucille is pregnant again. And those kids are so skinny. They can't be feeding them enough." Uncle Dick's rich baritone rumbled into my ears. "Well Frankie, some folks just . . ." The sound was muffled, but I knew that my uncle and aunt referred to my parents and my family's position as the "poor relations."

I also guessed the reason for the sniffling I heard from my uncle and aunt's bedroom: I had heard Mom refer to Aunt Frankie as "barren." I suspected that meant she could not have children because she often ended visits with our family by imploring my parents to give her one of their children to rear. In my eyes Aunt Frankie certainly didn't look "barren" because she had an exquisitely beautiful "high yella" face and a body that seemed to curve in all the right places—if the women in *Jet* or *Ebony* were the standards—although my dad pointed out unkindly that she had "bird legs." Hiding in one of my favorite eavesdropping locations, a closet, I had also overheard my mom say that her brother could not be the reason for Aunt Frankie's failure to have children because he was "so fine and all the women love that tall Black man."

With no children of their own, my aunt and uncle had volunteered to keep me during the first two years of my life because my parents had worked in "service" as a maid and chauffer for rich White folks in a neighboring Illinois city. This service job meant that they stayed at their employer's home for at least six of every seven days each week. My aunt and uncle's tenure as my caregivers ended when Mom and Dad decided to move from the Chicago suburbs to rural Michigan to make a go of farming. They took me with them.

My recollections were interrupted when the deep, deep rumbling of Uncle Dick's voice broke through to me again. "Hush, Frankie! You'll wake them up . . ." Well, little did they know, it was too late for that for me. Meanwhile, I glanced across the double bed that my two younger sisters occupied with me while we were "on vacation" in Illinois. I quickly closed my eyes as I heard footsteps in the hallway. I told myself to breathe normally, to act like I was asleep as the door slid gently open and shut on the three of us in our "uninterrupted slumber."

Soon the shower water ran next door in the bathroom and I relaxed, opened my eyes, and thought more about what I had heard. I felt mortified and deeply ashamed of my parents' success at having babies even though as the first child, I surely was not to blame.

Why did this early morning conversation generate such strong and long-lasting emotions? Upon reflection more than five decades later, I realize that my ultimate discomfort and deeply-felt sense of shame from overhearing this conversation had a great deal to do with the specific era of the 1950s, a period of secrets where public propriety about private behavior was the standard. I had just overheard a deeply-held secret that seemed to be an indictment of my parents' lower-class sex life and fertility: They had too many children to feed on one labor's paycheck. I sense now that my Aunt Frankie was very hurt by her inability to bear children and that she had hoped to raise me as her own. I think that perhaps she believed that all her middle-class achievements (although because they owned rental property and a business they would have been considered upper class in the African-American community) did not make up for a non-productive sex life and children of her own. She and my uncle could only be occasional substitutes or babysitters when it suited other family members.

My Uncle Dick and Aunt Frankie's conversation put my family's lower-class poverty in a negative light. This is was why I cried for days afterward and why my father took me on a shopping trip to a local department store to cheer me up. After he looked at my sad face and got me to admit the situation, Dad said, "Don't mind Aunt Frankie. She means well, but sometimes she just talks too much. What if I take you shopping for a new summer outfit? You won't ever have to stay there again unless you ask to do so." I quickly agreed to the shopping trip, and it helped me to forget (almost) the shame of overhearing my relatives' negative comments about my family's poverty. This event was the end of my overnight visits at Aunt Frankie and Uncle Dick's home again until I got married almost 20 years later. I have a very long memory for slights.

Although I may not have realized that our family was poor, I did know that our relatives in Evanston, Illinois, were very helpful to us. Uncle Harry or Aunt Goldie might say, "Frank and Lucille, I saw this chair (or radio, coat, curtains, or toy) that someone threw away in the rich neighborhood so I brought it for you to look at—I thought you might be able to use it." There are a number of pictures of Gail and Frances in our older cousins' clothing, and they look very pretty. At the time I understood these transactions as just a sensible way to prevent waste of items that we could use and others could not. I adopted this same approach to my own life, especially after I found out that Uncle Harry and Aunt Goldie, who I judged to be quite affluent because they owned large well-appointed homes with big lawns in the suburbs of Chicago, also picked up rummage to use. I reasoned that if it was okay for such family members, then it was okay for me to wear or use. Likewise, I learned to dress fashionably and shop on sale from Aunt Goldie: wear K-Mart underwear that you get on sale while you sport a marked-down dress from Saks Fifth Avenue or Marshall Fields. Better yet, sew a dress with a fancy pattern at a fraction of the cost.

"Please pass the sugar . . . thank you," we kids learned to say. My mother was very conscious of the "correct" way of doing things because she had been instructed in upper-class behavior by her foster mother, Gladys Adams, who took over from Aunt Johnnie some time in Mom's fourteenth year. My father wanted his children to someday become upper-class, and my mother's etiquette instruction supported this. We always sat down to eat, had paper napkins, said grace, passed the food, waited until everyone else was served, usually turned the television off, and asked to be excused if we finished eating before the rest of the family. While working at the University of Chicago, I attended a dinner where the table linen was a beautiful lavender color. I commented on the linen to my boss as he said, "In a month I will leave this job." I was so shocked that I picked up the wrong fork and began to eat. He chastised me by saying, "Is the tablecloth so beautiful that you have forgotten to wait for the guests of honor to begin eating first? By the way, that is the wrong fork for the appetizer." I was embarrassed, and I knew that if my mother had seen me she would have been too.

Not knowing how to behave and look in an upper-class situation can be an obstacle for first-generation college graduates. If your lack of "know-how" in social situations announces your background, then you can be stereotyped or devalued for a behavior that has nothing to do with your merit. This is one of the reasons that many McNair Scholars and other anti-poverty programs offer etiquette classes for their students, and the students learn such behaviors as commonly accepted table manners and how to conduct themselves in a formal business setting. If you master these social conventions, then you will eliminate one aspect of arbitrary "differences" that may separate you, however slightly, from your career goals.

In the senior year of high school I was crowned "Miss Van Buren County Community Center." I had a sponsor, Mrs. Thomas, who was determined that I win because she told my parents, "Betty is well spoken, a Christian girl from a good family, and she has always been on the Honor Roll. We need someone like her to represent Negro people." So Mrs. Thomas held fundraisers and pestered folks in church to buy the ten-cent votes necessary to elect me to the position. I reached out to my very large extended family for support and got a few kids I knew to put in their dime votes. I read a poem I had written for English class and modeled a formal dress. After this the votes were counted. I really did not expect to win because the other contestants were much more popular than I. Shockingly, I did win. However, I have always believed that it was because at the last minute the most popular girl withdrew from the competition. Nevertheless, the following year I returned to crown the new queen, and just as I got up from my chair, the slip that I had made for the occasion dropped to the floor. I gasped, but my mother who was right behind me whispered, "Keep going, smile, I got this," she said, whipping the slip into her purse. I walked on stage as though nothing had happened and crowned the new queen as the sixty-odd people in the audience applauded. My mother taught me that if you keep your cool, you can handle almost anything—including losing your underwear in a public place.

Racism

The United States Constitution recognized African Americans as less than human—three fifths of a man. Even with the abolition of slavery in 1865 under the 13th Amendment to the Constitution, dominance of the White race over those of African heritage continued through lack of federal, state, or local law enforcement; creation of state and local laws to undercut racial equality; and traditions of racial bias and prejudice in education, housing, employment, religion, and social interaction. Taken together, these legal and social conventions have resulted in a disproportionately low percentage of African Americans who earn high incomes and, until the 1980s, a lower-than-expected number in the middle income group. Racism has also served, in many instances, to divide working-class people who might otherwise find common ground to seek a "greater piece of the pie."

My son and daughter learned about racism much as I did: from childhood experiences. Unlike sexism, which Friedan (1963) first discussed in *The Feminine Mystique* as it related to the unhappy marital lives of her Smith College friends, thus sparking the modern women's rights movement, racism is a fact of life that most Blacks are introduced to as children.

A young relative, Kimberly Freeman, recently told me, "Well, we are used to being racially discriminated against; it is a fact of life. It just does not seem as awful as sexual discrimination, which is very personal in a physical way." Kimberly's comments remind me of a terrible habit I had as a child: When I was hurt and the injury began to heal, I picked the scab off repeatedly. Somehow each time that I picked the scab off, the wound didn't seem to hurt as much anymore. Maybe being hurt racially is like that scab: The wound no longer hurts so much when it is reinjured. Perhaps also these comments reflect the movement of our society from a strict caste system that my ancestors left behind in Kentucky and Texas, to one in which there is somewhat more economic opportunity although with an outsized proportion of Black poor. Although we Blacks generally believe that there is need for a great deal more economic and social progress, our White sisters and brothers often argue, "Now we have a Black President, Governor of Massachusetts, and Oprah Winfrey as one of the richest women in the country, you are equal. What more do you want?" The work of Brown people is more likely to support the wealth of the affluent, despite notable exceptions, because they are not compensated enough to purchase the necessities of life. During the late 1990s and early 2000s when I traveled to other countries such as Brazil, France, the Czech Republic, and Great Britain, I was astounded to learn that the United States does not have the corner on solving social problems. Instead, some other countries guarantee food, education through college, housing, and health care as rights.

Equally surprising to me was the fact that *all* citizens had these rights and that, on average, they lived longer than most Americans. The ability to meet basic needs such as food, housing, and medical care apparently can be accomplished within a country that is less based on class exclusion and historic discrimination. In my opinion, Brown people in this country want to have our basic needs met and an equal chance to do better than that based on our talents.

As my parents had with me, I had to explain racism to both my children at a young age because their White playmates ostracized them because of their race. In my son's case, one day he came home after second grade in tears as he explained that the little White girls in his class told him he couldn't sit with them at the lunch table. I asked what had happened before they said this, and he looked at me with big brown sad eyes and told me that he had wanted to play with them on the playground, and they said, "No, you can't. Go away because we don't like you." Then they all stormed off in a group and left him alone. He had known and played with many of these girls since pre-school. I asked the school social worker to investigate, and she observed the children's interaction and reported back, "It is as much that he is a boy as that he is Black." While the social worker intervened with the children and their families to assure that the girls would stop taunting Jahi and become aware of their insensitivity, I had to explain to him, "Son, some people will not like you because you have brown skin." He said, "Why is that?" I replied, "Because they think that they are better than us because they are White." Jahi said, "That is a stupid way for anyone to think." This is still his opinion of racism.

My daughter was also racially taunted in elementary school. She cried and begged me not to interfere. There was nothing that could stop me from marching into the principal's office to report the incident. He reddened, apologized, and said that he would look into it. As a Black parent, I felt helpless to explain the illogic of racism to my young children. So I recalled for them some of my earliest childhood memories when I first learned about racial hatred. "I was asleep and some of the neighbors came in the middle of the night to set a fire behind my family's home in southwestern Michigan." Jahi said, "What did Grandpa Brown do about that?" I recalled, "He took his shotgun and shot in the air over the arsonists' heads. The neighbors never returned. This is why you must not start a fight, but you must protect yourself if those girls or anyone else tries to physically hurt you." Another childhood story that I told both Jahi and Aisha: "Once I had a playmate who invited me to her home, and I had great fun exploring the woods and animal pens on her farm. While petting her shiny black cat, I asked, 'What's his name?' She told me, 'Nigger.' That was our last play date." From my old wounds, my children were taught to fight if someone tried to physically hurt them, and to never put up with anyone who belittles you racially. In some instances one has to ignore verbal abuse or ostracism, and in others challenge it through established procedures. There is no good way to explain prejudice and racism; I am a Black parent who just did what I felt I had to do to protect my young offspring.

Sexism: Assault, Rape, and Harassment

By *sexism* I mean actions, traditions, and laws that prevent women from having equal standing in society politically, economically, or socially. Such actions may be perpetrated by men or women to maintain a status quo where men are often favored. The results of individual conformity of action are large-scale social outcomes such as a disproportionate number of poor who are women with children or the inequality of the average women's to men's earnings (approximately 81 cents to a dollar in 2010). Generation after generation has supported social standards of behavior that create a lesser status for women as a group within the overall society so that women are often reared to take care of a doll baby and to be passive in the face of aggression. As an adult employee, the same woman may be criticized when she pursues a career and may be expected to be quiet about inequality of income in the workplace.

There is a very dark hole of memory where I have hidden scary bad things that make my heart race with fear and anger while my eyes tear with remembered pain and humiliation. These memories are of instances when I have been a victim of assault, when I was raped, and when I was sexually harassed on the job because I am a woman. I am calling the perpetrators Tom, Dick, and Harry.[9] My black hole of memories dates from the 1970s when there were no assault centers, rape hot lines or crisis programs, no federal, state, or local laws regarding sexual harassment. One of my dear friends, whom I will call Sally, a wise-cracking, brilliant lesbian, explained the role of sexism to me during the early 1970s. She said, "The basis for sexism is that men don't tend to assault other men because they are afraid of getting their ass beaten. Men are almost always stronger than we are, so if it comes to hand-to-hand combat, then they are more likely to win. They rely on the 'might makes right' adage to dominate us physically, psychologically, and professionally because again they believe that being the stronger of the species, they belong at the top of the hill. The workplace custom that the flunky jobs must go to women is just an extension of their sexual dominance based on physical strength. We have just got to stop accepting this shit."

These comments did explain some of the mysterious actions of men to me. I recalled one beast that I had known in college, Tom, a law student who maneuvered to have his roommates leave us alone after I had traded the guys free food for my cooking skills. Tom was a handsome brown man who stood at least 6' tall to my 5'7" and outweighed me by about 50 pounds.

---

[9] These accounts of assault, rape, and harassment are not intended to involve any person living or dead; any resemblance is purely coincidental.

As I turned to leave the apartment after the communal meal, I heard the door close as the others left me alone with Tom. He lunged at me instantly and breathed out his invitation, "Let's have a little after-dinner dessert." I said, "No." As we fought, we crashed into chairs, tables, and lamps, until finally Tom pushed me onto the living room couch where I continued to squirm, punch, kick, and yell. I absolutely did not want to lose my virginity to this lout who seemed to believe that being handsome with good career prospects gave him the right to my body. Eventually Tom let me go as he gasped almost sadly, "You are a strong old country girl. When I do pin you down, then I won't be able to perform because of all this fighting." Of course I had no sympathy for this wannabe rapist, so I scrambled up and got out of that apartment. The next time I encountered a rapist, I would not be so lucky.

My father and mother had always told me, "Never let a man put his hands on you. Don't allow anyone who claims to care for you to hurt you. Demand respect." When they said these words, I was in my late teens. I had never encountered a man who wanted to force himself on me. Living in rural southwest Michigan, separated by 10 long miles from boys my age, in the company of caring adults almost every waking hour of my day meant that I had only gone on a handful of dates. By my parents' standards I got the respect of all the boys I had dated. They did not pursue further physical contact when I indicated that we should stop at a kiss and caress. With the exception of Tom, the other men that I met in college and shortly after relied on their "sweet talk," fun dates, personality, or good looks as encouragement for sexual favors.

Harry proved Jane's point about physical dominance. Harry had a two-degree black belt in karate; numerous large glittering trophies were prominently displayed in his living room. Standing just a head taller than me, Harry was a stunningly beautiful very Black man who sported an Afro to die for: huge, jet-black, and with a few beautiful waves at the nape of his neck. He always

110

wore a colorful dashiki shirt and possessed personality plus. He was also a prominent social worker to my junior status, and he flattered me with attention and dazzled me with his sophisticated knowledge of our profession and all of the Black Power advocates that he knew. The only reason that I did not want to pursue a relationship with Harry was because he was an associate of a guy that I was already involved with. Surrounded by African statues and photographs of famous people that Harry knew, we sat in his living room one afternoon and argued amiably about Black Power ideology and what it implied for social work. Suddenly Harry kissed me. I put out my hands and reminded him about his associate; Harry just ignored everything I said. The situation ended when Harry raped me. The old country girl was just not strong enough to fight off a karate champion.

When it was over, I unleashed an hour or two of verbal bullets, slaps, and punches on Harry. He cried and said, "Hit me; I deserve it. I really feel miserable, and I thought I would feel good now. I am ashamed of myself." I think that he should have felt the remorse before the act. There was absolutely no question of calling the police because it was not done during that era: If they even came they would just see us as two squabbling young Black people. I knew that they would not have believed that a crime was committed. This is similar to the situation that so many women have been in.

To this day I remain angry and frustrated that I was not strong enough to prevent the rape and to whip Harry's ass. We did not become lovers. As a result of the violent rape, the bruises and cuts, I just could not continue to see Harry's associate either because I just could not keep this secret or risk the possibility that the two men would tangle. In retrospect, I believe that I became more concerned about my boyfriend's life than my honor. I had miscalculated a man's (granted someone that I admired) desire to physically dominate me and overestimated my own capacity to protect myself. I did not want what happened and have never felt a moment's guilt.

I ended my relationship with both Harry and his associate shortly after this incident.

Dick, my supervisor, showed me that men's physical dominance or the threat of physical dominance can extend to the work place; he practiced sexual harassment before it became cool. This was decades before congressmen left office because they had abused their positions of power to obtain sexual favors from subordinates. It was way before movies portrayed the storyline that sexually tying a person's livelihood to work functions as a source of entertainment. The media, hence the public, discovered the phenomenon when my story and that of several other women became one of four documented in a film titled *The Power Pinch,* filmed in the early 1980s and distributed nationally. It preceded enforcement standards by government and private industry.

"Listen, Dick, you have been raving about this girl's skills since she started work," yelled the Personnel Director (more recently the title would be Human Resources Director) for our department. "So now at the end of her probation you want to give her an unsatisfactory evaluation and extend her probation? Well, I will not be a part of this. You have no proof. Not only have I heard you praise her, your senior staff has too. She brought in copies of your written notes that show you said she was excellent up until last week. Whatever your issues are with her, I will not support you on this! This meeting is over." This loud exchange occurred during my evaluation conference, and I was shocked but pleased that the Personnel Director, Mr. Amadeus, had been so blunt about Dick's objections to my becoming a permanent employee.

Stephen, the assistant director of the bureau, interpreted the situation for me. "Dick thought that you would want to go to bed with him." I found the thought of this disgusting and said so. "He has been talking about you a lot, maybe too much for this about-face . . . mentioning that you were a good employee and that he thought you were a fine-looking young woman. In fact, remember when he touched you during staff meeting that time?" I nodded affirmatively, but I was embarrassed to recall the situation when during a staff meeting, Dick had mentioned the differences he saw between men and women as they reacted to drugs; then he reached out to push his hand into my waist to demonstrate that a soft woman's body could not withstand the amount of drugs that a man's body could. From that day forward I avoided Dick, and during subsequent staff meetings, my Black male colleagues sat flanking me so he could not get to me without touching them first. This is why Stephen inquired, "Sorry to ask this, but are you interested in him?" When I replied negatively, then he and my other male colleague told me how to protect myself in the event that Dick decided to relate my lack of interest in him to my job performance. This is why I had copies of all the assignments I had been given along with Dick's handwritten comments. I had a set of these papers at home and at the office where they were locked in a cabinet. My two senior colleagues also said that they would report "exactly what we have seen." They meant that they would confirm that I had done good work and that I had shown no interest in Dick. Furthermore, they had told me to keep a daily log of all my contacts with anyone as related to the job and to produce it or use it as evidence when or if Dick made any threats about my job. Their advice saved my job. I was taken off probation and given the excellent rating substantiated by all my supervisor's written statements. Shortly after this I applied for and received a transfer to the city's civil rights department.

"I was born this way . . . we are all born superstars," wisely sings the 2011 super-hot recording artist Lady Gaga (nee Stefani Germanotta). My parents gave me much the same positive sense of self despite the devaluation that American society places on those born like me: out-of-wedlock, African-American heritage, poor, and a woman. Lady Gaga's song sold over 20 million copies within its first months of release because she touches even such unlikely devotees as me and other women who are eligible for retirement as we happily dance to this jumping tune in the exercise classes we take with much younger folks. Lady Gaga's unconditional proclamation of acceptance for her listeners helps them to believe that this super-talented and wealthy performer in her outrageous costumes (remember the dress made of raw meat?) understands what it means to be an outsider, an imposter to greatness, within American society. While many believe that this song is focused exclusively on members of the gay, lesbian, and transgender community, when I am dancing (and sweating profusely) to the driving beat I believe that the singer is cheering *me* and other first-generation, brown, and low-income scholars on as we try mightily to live up to our potential.

In seventh grade I read a book about George Washington Carver, the famous African-American inventor who had been born into slavery yet credited with over 100 inventions derived from peanuts and sweet potatoes. I have a lifelong hobby of reading about diverse individuals who have solved problems of racism, feminism, or classism. People like the first African-American U. S. Supreme Court Justice, Thurgood Marshall; former chairwoman of the Federal Deposit Insurance Cooperation, Sheila Blair; co-founder of *MS Magazine*, Gloria Steinem; former presidents Abraham Lincoln, Harry Truman, and Bill Clinton; current president Barack Obama; scientist Marie Sklodowska-Curie also know as Madame Curie; educators Booker T. Washington, Vernon Polite, and Luis Rodrigues. For me their stories demonstrate that no matter how society perceives you, you can still build on your natural gifts and achieve.

From a practical standpoint, the tales of these folks' lives have inspired me since adolescence as I dealt with the co-requirements of my birth characteristics such as the inability of my parents to provide for all of my primary needs like medical or dental care (classism), the overt racial discrimination of physical attack on the school grounds by White playmates (racism), or as a young adult who was harassed by a White male supervisor seeking sexual favor (sexism).

References

Brown-Chappell, B. (1991). *The Black movement model of mayoral leadership. Ph.D. diss. University of Chicago.*

Friedan, B. (1963). *The feminine mystique.* New York, NY: Norton and Company.

Nocera, J. (2011, July 10). Sheila Blair's bank shot. *New York Times Magazine*, 24L. Retrieved from http://www.nytimes.com/pages/magazine

Chapter 6 — The Nuts and Bolts of Gettin' Over: The Doctoral Program

Although my graduate school teachers tried to interest me in doctoral studies, by the time I had a master's degree, I was tired of school, wanted to pay off my student loan debt, make some money, and most importantly have fun. However, in my late thirties, I was employed in higher education without the "union card" of a PhD. One day a dean from the University of Illinois at Champaign consulted for my university and told me that in his judgment I should obtain a doctorate. He said, "Those who have what it takes owe it to the rest of us to excel." The dean, a physically imposing ebony figure whose deep bass voice sounded to me like the voice of eternity, was a well-regarded African-American pioneer in social work education. Others had told me that I could obtain a doctoral degree, but this man, in a position to know what it took to succeed, also appealed to my sense of duty to others. I had advocated for others at all levels of government, but with this dean's words the doctoral program began to represent a new arena to fight—a national intellectual arena where few African Americans had been successful.

On the face of it, I was not a good candidate to attend the University of Chicago, the most prestigious (and probably the most expensive) school of social work in the country: I was an older married student with financial obligations and little disposable income but a lot of debt. I had two very young children, and I had "statistics anxiety." My "statistics anxiety" came from the fact that I had never studied trigonometry (which is very helpful to understand statistics) and had taken my last math class about twenty years earlier. Despite these apparent drawbacks, I began to seek information about admission.

Even without the doctoral degree I had served as president of a number of state-wide organizations, testified before Congress, published articles in a professional journal, and presented at numerous national, state, and local conferences. Green University had granted me tenure and promoted me to the position of a Program Director. I believed that I was on my way up the academic ladder, until the university's provost (chief academic personnel officer who reports to the president) told me that I should plan to hang out on the middle rung of the ladder for the rest of my career: Program Director was as far as I would advance at Green University or anywhere else unless I had the PhD, a means to climb further up the ladder.

A Salvador Dali print helped me to make the final decision to apply for doctoral studies. The president of Green University, the first Black in this position, had a reception for faculty at his home. As I washed my hands in the president's immaculate guest bathroom, out of the corner of my eye I spied an unusual piece of art; I was amazed to find Dali's surrealist flourishes of bright colors mashed together with black slashes hung in a modest gilt frame to one side of the sink. I squinted to see the artist's signature where the print number was tucked into a corner of the work. To own a numbered and signed print represented exceptional wealth and status to me. This Black man had clearly "gotten over." Later, as I passed through the receiving line, met this affluent and accomplished Black man in person, I was encouraged tenfold. I seemed to be living the images of *Ebony* magazine stories of success that I had read since childhood. The situation energized me in the same way that Chicago's Reverend Jesse Jackson's sermons did when he preached, "I am somebody! I may be poor. I may be Black, but I am somebody!" I thought that even if I did not obtain the exact position and wealth that Green University's president had, if I armed myself with a doctoral degree from a prestigious university, I would gain more skills in advocacy and access to decision-makers. I could have a much greater impact on the social welfare of underrepresented and poor people than I had in my current position.

Thus inspired, I quickly began to prepare my doctoral applications. When I explained to a White neighbor (doctoral-degree faculty member at another university) that I planned to apply to both the University of Michigan and Chicago, she frowned and said: "Don't get your hopes up because they are among the best in the country." I replied to my neighbor—borrowing a phrase from President Jimmy Carter—"Why not the best?" My motivation to attend these prestigious universities was not altered one bit by my neighbor's well-meaning comment; I think she underestimated me due to my race. Despite this comment, I was on a mission to achieve and become a much more qualified advocate for the people whom I cared deeply about.

I also judged that I had a good probability of admission to these schools because I already had two degrees from Michigan and had maintained contact with several nationally-respected faculty members who agreed to serve as my references. I had been admitted to both for my Master of Social Work degree. Each university had faculty who were respected researchers and authors in my area of interest, social welfare policy leadership. Last, although I was not aware of it at the time, my preliminary study of Harold Washington's mayoral win in Chicago, which I had reported at a national conference that year, demonstrated to the doctoral admission committees that I had the discipline to do research.

Within weeks of my applications, I was admitted to both schools. I chose Chicago because it did not require a move for my family and the dean concurrently offered me an administrative post (with more money than I had been earning) as the Assistant Dean of Recruitment and Enrollment. The combination of these two offers made me ecstatic. I remember that for the first weeks of work my car seemed to fly through the sunrays from my suburban home, tracing a path south onto Lakeshore Drive as I looked out over the bluest blue of Lake Michigan in a happy haze of excitement and anticipation for good things to come. Arriving on campus I would gaze across the wide expanses of manicured lawns where imposing gray buildings were guarded by ancient mythical animals, gargoyles, and think superstitiously, "Everything is so wonderful; life can only go down from here." It did.

The Dissertation Chair, Dr. Pastora San Juan Cafferty

It is a wonder that I graduated at all. When I first met Professor Pastora San Juan Cafferty in the narrow basement hall of the SSA (School of Social Service Administration) building the week before class started I asked, "Are you serious? There are over thirty-five books on your reading list for a ten-week term." Professor San Juan Cafferty, who was dressed elegantly in a tailored navy jacket and gray flannel slacks, regarded me skeptically, drew herself up to all five feet three inches of her height and clipped out, "My dear, you are at the University of Chicago." I got to work on reading those books that very afternoon, forcing myself to read the table of contents, introduction, conclusion, and then to skim remaining chapters. I disciplined myself to read very fast (65-100 pages an hour) and to underline and dog-ear passages that I could quote in class to strengthen my points when I offered an answer or posed a question. I read all 35 books in ten weeks because I was more scared to fail than I was of the challenge laid before me. Once I began to read the books, I found the material for her class on urban politics in Chicago to be provocative and engrossing; in class I even began to suggest further sources from my own research.

I also developed a parlor trick that I still use as a professor: If I want to emphatically make a point, then I memorize the page numbers and specific paragraph placement for the material. This impressed my teachers as it still does my students. My efforts seemed to pay off because I earned an *A* in Dr. San Juan Cafferty's class, took a second course with her, and she agreed to become my dissertation chairperson. [10]

In my first year at SSA I met with my advisor (responsible to recommend coursework and to help the student with informal and formal expectations of doctoral work) in her small box of an office where a giant fichus tree grew along the ceiling and overshadowed us both. Professor Dolores "Dodie" Norton, a whisper-thin African-American scholar, was also a good friend of Pastora's; she told me how to best get along with her as the chairperson of my committee: "If she asks for something—your proposal, a chapter, a hearing date—then do everything you can to meet her requests. If you have any difficulties with deadlines,

---

[10] The dissertation chairperson at Chicago, and most universities, directs the student's research work. This includes oversight of the cumulative knowledge tests often called specialized or general examinations. Following the examinations, the chairperson gives preliminary approval for the dissertation (research) topic, guides the student's preparation of the dissertation proposal, schedules the proposal hearing, conducts the hearing, informs the student and school of the results, and reviews progress on the dissertation. After reading early drafts of the dissertation, the chairperson schedules the dissertation hearing, conducts it and announces the hearing results to the student and university units; he or she also signs all required paperwork to document the student's achievement throughout the course of study. This person is extremely important to the student's subsequent job search as they traditionally provide suggestions for jobs and references to obtain jobs.

and try not to, then let her know beforehand. She enjoys your area, leadership and mayors, a great deal, and once she knows that you are dependable and will work hard, she will get you out of here. She has an excellent record of helping students to graduate. Remember, her time is very limited—she serves on a major corporate board and is involved with many civic organizations—so always be on time, but do not take offense if she runs late; that is just the way it is for students. Finally, let her call the shots about others who will be part of your committee."

Thank goodness I followed Dr. Norton's advice about how to relate to Dr. San Juan Cafferty. It came in very handy when several other very famous faculty members surprised me and announced that they intended to either be on my committee or to chair it. One "gentleman" even told me: "You will be totally under my power when I am chairman of your committee." I sucked in my stomach, pulled myself up to my full height, looked him straight in the eye, and said as sternly as I could muster, "Remember, you are a member of the Committee. Pastora is the Chairperson." The "gentleman" seemed somewhat taken aback, but under no circumstance did I want him as the chairperson despite his expertise: As chairperson this "gentleman" had recently required one of my classmates to extend his dissertation revisions for over a year when it normally took only a month or so.

Traditionally, the dissertation chairperson is considered the "boss" of the dissertation and manages not only the procedural details and the student, but also the other members of the committee, who often defer to the chair in disputes with each other or the student. When I recommended other committee members, as chairperson, Pastora would accept or veto my suggestions. Once she told me, "You can have that person on the committee, but I will resign." I did not ask the other faculty member to join the committee. Over the years, we met one or two times per semester to discuss my specialized examination, research, or dissertation. Pastora said, "The only good dissertation is a done dissertation." I was in total agreement.

To me both the general and specialized courses seemed like an excellent chance to write papers that were related to my area of research interest. (Professor Steve Burghardt at Hunter College had told me before I entered SSA to write about my topic every opportunity that I got, and it proved to be very helpful.) It took me about two years to finish the general courses and pass that examination and another year to complete the specialized courses. Ultimately, I enjoyed writing the Specialized Examination in the two weeks allotted by my faculty. Six months later I revised and added to the content of the Specialized Examination so that the material formed the basis of my dissertation proposal. I then successfully defended the proposal (i.e. presented a summary of my proposed research and answered questions on the material).

Despite my initial mistake to question the reading assignments in her class, Pastora and I grew to respect the machinery of each other's minds. I was intrigued by her endless knowledge of Chicago politics and urban planning. She and "the gentleman" asked to see all sixty-five of my interview transcripts as soon as they were complete.[11] They enjoyed the new perspectives that these interviews with former mayors, congressmen, social workers, business people, city council members, media types, and other academics provided them. On many occasions we all laughed at some of the ridiculous behaviors my interviewees exhibited while I spoke to them. For example, a congressman leaned his large buttocks back in his

---

[11] The transcripts of the sixty-five interviews are available at the Chicago Historical Society under the title, "Betty Brown Chappell Interviews of Chicago Politicians and Officials," and a smaller subset of transcripts plus my dissertation are housed at the Charles H. Wright Museum in Detroit.

very rickety but small office chair, retrieved a hand mirror and began plucking in-grown hairs from his face during the interview. He never even asked if I wanted to rest my coat or sit down in his little hole-in-the wall office even though the heat was blasting.

When Pastora had to cancel some of our individual meetings or cut the time short, then I remembered what Dr. Norton, my advisor, had told me about the role of a doctoral student and did not resent it. This challenged me many times. At Pastora's request we rearranged our discussion of my proposal for a day that had a very bad snow storm; she was late for the meeting. When Pastora was available she told me that I had fifteen minutes or I might have to reschedule a couple of months in the future. I took a deep breath and summarized what I had to say very quickly. At the end she told me that she was satisfied, and we could proceed to a full hearing of my proposal. Then she promptly excused herself to attend a meeting about a Chicago bid for the Olympics; the city is a perpetual bridesmaid. I left her office exhausted but elated at my progress.

In the spring of 1991, I was poised to defend my dissertation and assume an academic position. Then disaster struck: Pastora's husband died in a car accident, and she was injured. Days later, during his wake, as she stood at the end of his beautiful mahogany casket, this wonderful and brave woman put her grief aside and said, "Don't worry, I am going to get you out this summer." She reviewed all my drafts for the dissertation hearing, then chaired the committee in late June of 1991, despite what surely was an extraordinarily difficult and sad time for her.

Even so, I was the one who cried when she announced, "Congratulations Dr. Brown-Chappell." The "gentleman" asked me why was I crying, and I told him. "Well, this has been so difficult. Two of my relatives died this spring. Then a couple of weeks ago you wanted me to stay enrolled to do more revisions. My husband and children are waiting to move so I can take my new job in Michigan. Jahi (my fourteen-year-old son) got run into by a car this month. He is all right now, yet I had to stay here and revise my dissertation while his dad took him to the hospital." With this last statement everyone in the room had tears in their eyes. The "gentleman" said, "I am sorry." I replied, "It's okay, because last night I killed a roach on my extra copy of the dissertation. It's the one I just gave you when you said that you forgot yours. See those brown spots on the front?" He looked at the papers in surprise. Then he wiped the tears from his eyes, and everyone else did too. We all had a belly laugh then, and the tension and sadness of the situation dissipated.

At the graduation I paused for a moment in my maroon doctoral robe and black velvet beret, feeling numb from the effort. Then I crossed under the peaked three-story high sanctuary walls as my feet fit into the stone grooves worn into the floor of Rockefeller Chapel's stage by many others; the president called my name, and one of the SSA faculty placed the doctoral hood over my head so that it draped my shoulders and ran down my back. It was August 30, 1991, when President Hanna Holborn Gray completed the ceremony that made me the first person in my family to receive a doctoral degree.

Multiple Roles: Work and School

Lucky for me, the University of Chicago had a tradition of employees who earned their degrees while working full-time. Because of this tradition, most people accepted the fact that I was both an administrator and student; one moment I might be taking a class and the next I might ask my professor to cooperate with me on a recruitment task. I found this arrangement very awkward and had uneven results in handling the situation as these two roles were mixed into the thick soup of other roles in my life such as mother, wife, and sister.

Just prior to my first recruitment trip for SSA, I turned in my first assignment as a doctoral student. This was a crucial test for me. I was beset by doubts about my ability to achieve as compared to the younger students in my class. What if every other success in my life had been a fluke? What if I really wasn't that good? I didn't realize it at the time, but many doctoral students suffer these same doubts. Such doubts have been called "the imposter syndrome." With imposter doubts chasing around in my head, I became very anxious as I anticipated both the grade for this first assignment and possible problems with my first recruitment trip. In this state of heightened anxiety, my hands grew sweaty and my stomach got sick. I carried this fear of being an imposter like a lump of burning coal in my stomach while my husband and I gathered our children to make the three-hour journey to Holland, Michigan, for my first big job assignment. Apparently in the rush to complete the school assignment, pack up the kids, respond to my visiting brother about his romantic problems, bring my recruitment brochures, and make family travel plans, multiple role demands must have "overloaded my system." The morning of my appointment in Holland, I discovered that I had forgotten all my dress clothes. Oops.

Because we stayed with my parents, who lived near Holland, I hurriedly borrowed clothes from my mother. I was sure that I looked strange: My mother was five inches shorter than me and about thirty pounds heavier. However, no one seemed to notice my clothes as everywhere I went on my visit, people seemed to stare at my dark brown skin when I introduced myself to them as the Assistant Dean from University of Chicago. (This reaction may seem odd some twenty-five years after my visit to Holland, Michigan, but the area made news even in 2007 when nearby college students distributed a journalism project which had African Americans in blackface plus many other derogatory symbols.) When introduced to me in the cafeteria line, one tall gangly professor opened his mouth, fell over a chair, and watched in amazement as his tomato soup flew into the air and splattered on him and other diners. On a positive note, after this first visit the officials at this college enthusiastically cooperated with me by distributing SSA information and recommending students to me. Apparently they got over my funny clothes or brown skin or both. Upon my return to campus, I found out that I was not an imposter after all. I got the highest grade in my class on my first doctoral assignment.

Other times I did not understand the politics of the doctoral program. Some of my work relationships and conversations became a political liability for my future career.

"If you pass statistics and research course work, then the rest of the general coursework will probably pose no problem. The specialized coursework will be based on whatever you and your dissertation chair decide is necessary. This will certainly be material that you excel in." Thus said more advanced students. Coursework refers to about 15-20 classes that doctoral students take so that they can have a breadth and depth of knowledge in their field. In social work this means that all doctoral graduates should be able to knowledgably discuss major topics such as history, theories, research methods, and social work practice methods at the individual, group, family, community, or societal level. No matter how well you do in your general coursework, you know about some students whose bodies are buried beneath the school because faculty do not want them to live on as evidence of how difficult it is to pass the General (also known as Comprehensive) Examination which follows completion of general coursework. In some fields once the student has taken the general recommended or required courses, then they either sit for a written examination at a computer terminal for a day or two, or they are given some essay questions to finish at home within a specified time frame.

No matter what type of examination a student takes, the General Examination is another cause, among many, for fear of failure and some amount of competition. During my time at SSA, a group of about five of us decided to eliminate the competition, so we prepared for the General Examination using a reading list distributed by the faculty in addition to reviewing our notes and texts from some of our courses; we often met on a weekly basis to compare notes on the readings and to debate the issues raised in them. This process not only helped us to memorize the content of the 50-item reading list, but it also decreased the amount of isolation that most doctoral students suffer. On a number of occasions we took practice examinations using questions from previous Generals, had faculty give us feedback on our answers, or invited faculty to lead us in a discussion of specific books or articles.

In the spring term just prior to the General Examination, I confided in frustration to the dean, my supervisor, that Professor Jones (pseudonym) was not a very good teacher because she did not want to engage in dialog on substantive issues but rather made pronouncements about the content of our numerous textbooks. I thought this was a waste of students' time since many of the texts were on our General Examination reading list, and we needed to learn how to argue their merits so that we would be best prepared for the examination. Apparently what I thought was a private conversation with my supervisor went public very rapidly.

All the doctoral students who planned to sit for the examination took a course from Professor Jones in hopes that it would help us prepare for the big day. One day Professor Jones began class with a clenched jaw then squinted her bright blue eyes at me. Next she put her coat on, turned her back on the class and left abruptly, saying loudly, "Betty, why don't *you* take over the discussion? I am due at a meeting downtown." With that she hurriedly made her exit. I sat with my classmates in stunned silence until another student told me that Jones had just received word that the University of Chicago would not grant her tenure at SSA (a job for life with rare causes for dismissal like felony conviction or admitting to sexual harassment). Jones had graduated from SSA, taught for several years, published a well-received book and served as a staff person for a Congressional committee. With all of these accomplishments, my classmates told me that they heard that Jones's failure to get tenure was my fault. I knew this to be ridiculous because a single doctoral student, no matter what their administrative title or access to the dean, could not make comments that would outweigh all of Jones' other accomplishments. In fact, one of my faculty friends later explained to me that big prestigious schools like SSA are as well-known for who they tenure as for the many people they turn down. This is why Jones soon obtained an administrative post at another school. Apparently, the dean had used my comments as his excuse for a decision that he had wanted to make anyway. This political drama hurt my chances to apply for a faculty position at SSA because the dean later told me that Professor Jones' allies blocked any consideration of me as a candidate for a faculty position at SSA.

Another instance of political drama found me with foot-in-mouth disease at the dean's retirement party just a year before I graduated. My husband and I sat at the exclusive restaurant on Chicago's north side munching on overpriced food as the special guests of the dean; our location on the lakefront was so exclusive that the decorator had taken pains to make everything look like a seafront diner with barrels, nets, shells, and unpainted wood. There were no other doctoral students at this event. I had a few drinks (never a good idea in a work setting), and I felt comfortable with the faculty. That is why I took a chance with my "roast comments" to say, "The dean has been a commanding officer in the army and a leader at SSA, so we better not expect too much work out of him. With only a few weeks left, he's reverting to the good old army rules, FIGMO: F*** You, I Got My Orders!" Although the Dean laughed heartily at this, I heard later from a friend that the faculty members clucked secretly to each other, "She's not our type; she's too coarse—a lady should not curse in public. She is bright enough, but just too Black to be a faculty member here."

Obviously, I sometimes confused my dual roles as a student and administrator and the role expectations for my behavior while at SSA. From the situation with Professor Jones and the dean's retirement party, I learned to act differently until I graduated; doctoral students should be seen and not heard. Or if they are heard, they should be heard making only positive comments about faculty. *Nothing you say is confidential.* I also learned to never curse at social functions with faculty—until I graduated and got tenure myself. In any event, as a student and untenured faculty member you are always on probation for another job, a reference, scholarship, or some type of favor. I now know that when you become a faculty member the same holds true, but the stakes are not quite as high *once you get tenure.*

Multiple Roles: Family & Student

To balance all of the roles in my life (employee, mother, wife, student, sister, and friend) required a high tolerance for chaos. I studied while in my hotel room and while I flew or took the university car to the 35-plus colleges and universities on my annual recruitment itinerary. When not traveling, I studied on nights and weekends; I often stayed on campus overnight so that I could maintain total concentration. I had statistics anxiety so I waited to take the class until I had a strong grade point average to fall back on. I also took a non-credit statistics class before I enrolled in my doctoral statistics class; then I hired a statistics tutor and made virtually every office hour held by my statistics professor. I earned a *B+* in statistics, and I was elated. On the home-front, I missed many family events such as my sister's second wedding and some of my children's performances.

Assisted by our housekeeper, Lutichia Raggs, my husband worked and did *much* more than his share of night duty with the children. Mrs. Raggs, a mother and grandmother, was essential to our family's sanity, the children's safety, and our career and higher education goals. Good soldier that he was, Michael served as vice president of the PTA for a couple of years in order to guarantee that our kids were not overlooked for educational opportunities. An area of family discontent arose when Michael had to get the kids out to school while I traveled for work or studied on campus, and Mrs. Raggs was scheduled to work in the afternoon. Our daughter, Aisha, will tell you that this is one of her major complaints from those years. The braids her father fashioned for her looked a lot like antennae with barrettes on them.

On occasion, my efforts to balance the student-wife-friend-mother chaos just did not work. One weekend stands out as the worst case scenario. Some old friends arrived to visit us from Montana. The first indication that everything wasn't going smoothly is when I had to substitute a large orange squash for the Halloween pumpkin that I promised my son. Pressed for time as usual, I had waited too long to make the purchase, and the pumpkins were all sold out. Our friends' two very active boys fit right in the merriment of Jahi's birthday party on Friday night where they joined ten other boys who sang, ate pizza, and kept up a constant racket with games and toys. As the day ended, Michael returned from an international computer show that he had volunteered to manage after his work day and tiptoed through the darkened house past our guests (who were bedded down in the living room) to get a few hours' sleep before his Saturday assignment began.

The next day started out peacefully enough. Michael left before breakfast, and my visiting friend, Raymond, took charge of the three boys while his wife, Joyce, and I took Aisha to her ballet recital. We arrived and I looked proudly as Aisha, dressed in her beautiful pink ballet leotard and tutu, began her steps. However, for some reason my little cutie kept going the opposite way from all the other dancers. I was embarrassed, but Joyce seemed to take this all in stride. Then the teacher came over and whispered, "Mrs. Chappell, this is not Aisha's class." I collected Aisha, tried impossibly to hide my tall frame, and the three of us slunk out of the room. Aisha, sweet child, did not complain about my *faux pas* (wrong step); we returned a few hours later for the correct class—without Joyce.

Michael and I usually enjoyed taking out-of-town guests to one of our favorite French restaurants. Because my doctoral expenses were such a drain on our funds, going to this restaurant was a rare treat; we all felt special to escape our children and dress up as adults for a night on the town. Unfortunately, that evening, my husband was so exhausted from a hard week of work, managing the computer show and caring for our children with little help from me (I was perpetually studying), that he repeatedly fell asleep during dinner with our out-of-town guests. He was so tired that he did not stir even when I kicked him under the table. Looking over at me as I tried to awaken Michael while his head drooped once again upon his starched white shirt, Joyce said, "Don't worry about us; he must be tired." Her husband, an Episcopal minister, concurred. After this, the three of us ate our French food with relish; we even had dessert. Michael took his dinner home, and this dear understanding couple, the Browns (no relationship) has remained our friends to this day.

When I reflect upon this incident I am hot with embarrassment because I *know* my husband had an overload because he had agreed to do more than his fair share of parenting while also trying to further his own career. I am also beholden to my children, in this instance Aisha, because they were supportive of my goal to get a doctoral degree and have never criticized me even when they realized as adults the sacrifices that they had to make due to my miscues (like the ballet recital). The numbers of times that I was distracted or could not attend lunches, dinners, and special occasions in my friends' lives are too numerous to recount. At this vantage point I remain grateful for the ongoing love, affection, and understanding of all my friends and family.

Financial Nuts and Bolts

We refer then and now to this degree as *our* family's success because so much of our financial resources, time, and marital capital (time for each other) was invested in it. I received two lucky financial breaks that neither of us predicted at the outset of the risky journey. First, SSA's dean of students gave me an extra financial break: He did not enter my grades into the system until I had enough to register for a full course load. This arrangement meant that my overall costs for tuition were reduced even further when coupled with a one-half tuition benefit that I received as an employee. Second, I applied for and received some national (Delta Sigma Theta to the rescue again), state, and university fellowships (merit awards that required an *A* average). I also used my credit card liberally, racked up a truckload of interest debt, and cashed in some retirement securities. To devote more time to my research, I left my full-time job at Chicago during the last two years of my study and worked half-time for another university's extension program—fortunately located in the SSA building—where I continued to write my dissertation. Because my area of interest, social welfare policy at the local level, had no federal aid programs or private foundation support, unlike areas such as family and mental health practice, I needed money in these last two years for research costs such as copying, travel to interviews, books, equipment, and research assistants. Michael and I took a $15,000 second mortgage of our home for these expenses.

Pressure & Coping

"Betty, what is wrong with you in this picture?" asked my sister Frances, who is always perfectly groomed, as she recently thumbed through a family album. I looked over at the picture of myself dancing with an eight-year-old Aisha, who sports a toothy smile as we are caught by her dad's camera. I explained to Frances, "Oh. That was probably taken while I was writing the dissertation. I remember getting less than four hours sleep per night for months on end. I guess it shows in my face – those very dark raccoon circles around my eyes are from lack of sleep." I am not overweight because I was afraid that if I got too heavy Michael might be lured away from me. So I still worked out in aerobics class and ran with my neighbor (yes, the same White lady who thought I might not be admitted to U of C) while taking a low-dose of medication for hypertension. I motivated myself to keep my blood pressure under control by envisioning my husband's "future girlfriend" who would direct the children to take care of their mute, drooling vegetable of a mother. I knew that I did not want to have a stroke and be cared for by anyone else, but particularly by this fantasy girl friend. Thus, I might have been trim in the picture, but certainly not too attractive because who had time to get their hair styled? Not me. I stared a little closer at the picture and realized that my clothes were ugly and that my skin was rather blotchy. I felt sorry for my younger self. I could see why Frances was shocked at my appearance, which graphically showed the physical toll that the pressure to achieve had on me. My mental state was sometimes precarious also.

"A tisket, a tasket, I need a brain in my basket." Composing silly doggerel like this broke the tension to generate a first draft, then the constant rewrite of my research findings. Many days I would sit in my little 6' by 10' windowless doctoral office in the basement of SSA without insights or inspiration, rewriting my findings again and again, but failing to gain acceptance from Pastora. I discovered the calming effect of my silly verses one chilly dawn when I was in this little office and my industrious friend and Delta sorority sister, Earlie Washington, bounced by to tell me that she had coffee ready. She found me with tears of laughter running down my face. I showed her what I was writing and she said, "You are crazy. You better get started now." From that point on, I routinely wrote these silly statements and poems using the pen name of I. B. Blue. Once I wrote something silly, I was amused, it broke the tension, and I could continue to write the dissertation findings.

My troubles with writing stemmed largely from the two decades that separated my last college writing class and the SSA requirement for clarity in expression. (My writing as a social work practitioner and professor at Green University had served me well, but SSA's requirements were much more exacting.) Luckily, the committee agreed that I had discovered new knowledge because my research work offered *The Black Movement Model of Mayoral Leadership* as an alternate theory to understand Black mayors' leadership; I based it on 65 interviews, hundreds of newspaper articles, several videotapes, over 120 books and journal articles, plus government data and agency archives. However, as publisher of the premiere journal in our profession, SSA expects more than new knowledge. The school expects that all complex ideas must be expressed in a manner that an ordinary citizen can read: Every chapter contributes to the reader's ability to comprehend the total dissertation; every paragraph within every chapter enables the reader to understand the chapter; and every sentence in every paragraph contributes to the reader's ability to understand that paragraph. Thus, the dissertation must report knowledge that no one else has discovered, be clear, *and* interesting: hah!

A year later, after I had memorized the university's manual for authors and written and rewritten chapters, I concluded that I just could not produce the quality of writing that my committee expected of me. I asked my advisor, Professor Norton, for a suggestion, and she told me that some faculty and students worked with editors. I located an English instructor (she had a record of publication, a doctoral degree, and taught at the university) who agreed to serve as my editor.[12] I was willing to

---

[12] As a high school and undergraduate student, and then a professional social worker, my writing skills were considered quite appropriate: I was on the staff of the high school newspaper and after my master's degree had published professionally. The level of expectation is far greater the higher one goes in education. At the point I discuss here I had already taken a "Writing for Professionals" course, yet needed the help of an editor. Now I always work with both content and copy editors.

pay the editor's large hourly fee because the more that time ticked on without a viable draft, the more often that I saw attractive jobs filled by others. My family finances dictated that I get a full-time job. With the editor's help, after six months, I produced dissertation prose that my committee accepted.

During what became my last six months of writing, I have one particularly humbling yet vivid memory of my time at SSA, a time when I felt the weakest and least up to the intellectual, mental, and physical challenges posed by the doctoral program. In the last week of July 1991, I was desperately trying to complete a draft of my work for my dissertation hearing. At the time, I studied in the windowless basement computer lab. I had entered the program years earlier and had not had more than 20 hours of sleep in the previous seven days; my new job and my family's future plans depended on me holding it together. If I could finish the last draft of my dissertation that evening, then we would all leave Illinois for a new home, financial solvency, and friends in Michigan. We absolutely could not stay in a holding pattern much beyond that week.

Thoughts of failure rose up around me and transformed the neon-lighting to clouds of darkness. Since it was late at night there was no technology assistant available, and I was sure that the machines were my enemies; they would undoubtedly break down again and prevent me from making my deadline. I became sick to my stomach as I thought repeatedly, "No dissertation equals no job, no job equals no income for me, and financial hardship for my entire family." On legs that were numb from sitting for hours, I rose and stumbled to the bathroom down the hall, maybe trying to outrun my fears. I cried frantically in the stillness of the bathroom, and the sound echoed back, adding to my general hysteria.

I thought, "Maybe if you wash your face you can get a grip."

The cold water that I splashed on my face somehow evoked a soothing mental flashback: I was twelve and visiting my relatives in Evanston, Illinois. It was so early that the neighbors' windows remained shuttered as I peeked curiously out. A few cars rolled sleekly by, and the milkman in his delivery truck rumbled down the street with crates and bottles clinking in the quiet as the sun began to rise in the sky. To me as a child raised in rural Michigan, Evanston, Illinois—home of Northwestern University—was usually a very scary metropolis with strange people always moving about. I stayed with relatives who had a two-story bungalow surrounded by a small well-manicured lawn, but this home sat way too close to its neighbors for me. If you looked out at the right time, then you could see the neighbors as they moved about in their homes.

In my room a desk clock ticked away the time; I started to close my peephole when I spied a very old bent figure hobbling steadily forward. At first glance she seemed neither Black nor White, but certainly she was poor. On her bowed head was a dark woolen scarf, and as she advanced I could see her run-down black orthopedic shoes with huge blocky heels. Amazingly, her progress was not impeded by the fact that her knees seemed to point in opposite directions—beyond bowlegged. Her coat and skirt were so nondescript they seemed monochrome—maybe gray or beige, but not pretty at all. She carried a paper bag that I figured must be her lunch. Smoke curled from the cigarette in a corner of her mouth. If I strained my ears I could hear garbled sounds emanating from her mouth as she passed near the open screen of my window.

I was the only person to watch the old woman make her strange and painful walk. As she passed just under my window, I recognized her: She was my grandmother, Dad's mother; we called her Mama Metcalf once she remarried after Papa Brown's death. Later I learned that she passed this way three times a week walking to a nearby suburb where she cleaned a White lady's home and ironed the family's clothes. I had not recognized Mama Metcalf because I had never seen her in work clothes before. Whenever I had visited her home, located about a mile away, she had always been dressed up: She always had her hair "fried, dyed and laid to the side," as they say, and she wore lovely dresses with costume jewelry that my mother envied.

Although I was unaware of it during my early dawn vigil, Mama Metcalf apparently earned "a little spending change" by taking this sojourn. Her long walks undoubtedly financed the emergency loans that my father requested when his paycheck was short, paid for her lovely dress clothing, and once provided me with money to attend a summer camp sponsored by our church. As I continued watching Mama Metcalf, I recalled an earlier conversation when family members mocked her strange appearance on the way to work, "Mama is too old to smoke, and especially in public. That mumbling has to go too. She sounds crazy and she looks worse with those run over shoes and faded clothes." I was pleased, however, to see someone who loved me unequivocally pass by my window when I felt particularly lonely.

I returned reluctantly from my memories to the matter at hand: how to finish my dissertation. Splashing water on my face again, I mixed tears with water. I looked up. It seemed that I could see the reassuring and loving image of Mama Metcalf's long walk to work rise up unbidden. I said out loud, "I can do this." Now the sound of my voice reverberated strong and sure against the empty bathroom stalls. I began mumbling—much as she had done—coaching myself out of hysteria, then speaking stronger and more assertively: "If Mama Metcalf at seventy-plus could make that long walk on her spindly old legs to scrub, sweep, and iron so that her family would have some measure of financial security—even luxuries such as the summer camp—then I can certainly get through the next few days and graduate with this doctoral degree."

Since graduating from SSA with the doctoral degree in August 1991, I have regularly recalled Mama Metcalf's long and arduous walk to work. Other Black alumni have told me that I was only the twenty-first Black person to receive the doctoral degree from SSA since the degree's inception in the early 1950s. To me, her walk to work has come to represent strength and love because she looked so fragile, yet every day she seemed to defy others' expectations of decorum for a lady of her advanced years to do what she believed was essential: to be there financially whenever one of her children or grandchildren needed her. This thought of her love despite physical obstacles and criticism helped me do what at first seemed impossible.

I am constantly amazed when I hear social critics, media commentators, and politicians state that America has overcome racial and class obstacles. Given my family's humble educational, financial, and racial background, I have experienced both racial violence at the hands of Whites and the less obvious racism that yielded so few doctoral graduates in my discipline not only at the University of Chicago, but also nationally. These issues represent the types of obstacles that such critics, commentators, and politicians seem clueless about. Yet these issues are what belie the notions of equality in our society.

I believe that achievement is the result of a collective: family, friends, teachers, mentors, partners, neighbors, guardians, grandparents, and religious or spiritual advisors; the love that brought me through my educational obstacles humbles me, and I try to "pay it forward" to others as often as possible. I recognize that many students enrolled today do not have the same two-parent family foundation that I had, but I strongly believe that achievement is possible if such students actively seek and treasure mentors and support networks (church, neighbors, extended family, or counselors) that they do have on their journeys. Once I overheard one of my undergraduate students challenge another to "love and appreciate those who are holding you up; don't be sad for what you don't have, be happy for those who bless you with the love they have to give."

Chapter 7 — Tenure: The Game[13]

We often think of babies as powerless, but my baby was the deciding factor in my first positive tenure decision. Baby—and Baby's bowels, to be more specific—saved the day.

The majority of people who teach in a university or college that grants four-year degrees such as a bachelor of arts in sociology have earned a doctoral degree. A few, like me during my first academic jobs, are appointed with only a master's degree because they have extensive practice experience in their professional fields and have probably authored research reports, grant applications, or articles. While I met both of these requirements and was therefore a successful candidate for a faculty job, I was completely unfamiliar with the concept of "collegial" decision-making. I was an innocent.

My experience in social service agencies meant that I was accustomed to supervision by a single person called "boss." The

---

[13] When a faculty member receives tenure, that person has permanent employment and can compete for other promotions. This is serious business, but the notion of comparing the process to a game allows me to make some parallels that readers might find familiar.

boss (whom I knew personally) might take advice from others about my hiring, promotion, discipline, or firing, but the "boss" for all intents and purposes had the final say about my work and was responsible legally to make a decision within union rules and any pertinent laws. As was the case in my first employment situation, discussed in Chapter 5, when the "boss" made a mistake outside of the union rules and laws, then the Human Resources Office (called *Personnel* in my early career) could overrule such decisions. In contrast, in a collegial system like the one I first experienced at Green University, all of the other faculty in my department plus the director made recommendations to higher levels of the organization on my hiring, permanent status (called tenure), and promotion. By tradition, one or more of the higher levels (which may be called a University Personnel Committee, provost, president, or Board of Governors, sometimes called Regents) honor the recommendation of the department faculty and director. Final decisions are made by the Board of Governors (faculty rarely meet these folks) based on the recommendation of the provost (faculty have little or no contact with this individual) who is the highest personnel officer of the university. There is a method of appeal for negative decisions even in non-union colleges or universities.

Unlike my experience with the non-profit United Auto Workers Retired Workers Senior Centers or with the City of Detroit as a civil servant where probation lasted 90 days, probation at Green University lasted for three years, and each year prior to application for permanent status, the union's contract rules required me to submit an annual report. As this was my first experience with the tenure system of probation, I did not understand that my fellow workers had the authority and responsibility to evaluate me. I did not understand that case law allowed my colleagues to be arbitrary (without specific and consistent reason), yet their decision-making had to conform to the union contract, local, state, or federal laws in civil rights.

I often try to imagine what game is similar to the tenure system. I discard cards or Scrabble because unlike tenure, the rules in each of these games do not vary despite the number of times you play, who your opponents are, or the state where you play. A game that is reminiscent of tenure to me is the mystical role play game, Dungeons and Dragons (D and D), because the "Dungeon Master" is similar to the provost or chief academic officer whose staff explains and administers the rules. Also, each player creates a character with certain strengths and weaknesses related to the goal; this seems similar to the credentials a professor starts with and develops at a university. You start the game of tenure with credentials such as the prestige of the university you attended, regard of others in your field for your research, the number and importance of prior publications, and—in the field of social work—prior agency employment. All of these elements are somewhat in the eye of the beholder: One university might regard your publications as quite important because of the specific journal you published in, while another could find the same publication too "elementary." In D and D, as in tenure, there is a high degree of risk of death (in the game) or termination (in tenure). The more famous the university or college you work for, the higher the risk of "death" because many such institutions are known as much for the numbers and fame of those whom they terminate as for those whom they ultimately tenure (who are retained permanently and who "win the game").

When I began the tenure game, I was armed with a prestigious degree (meaning one from a large institution where the professors published a great deal), a couple of publications, years of practice experience, and moderate teaching evaluations. My application was also chock full of evidence of national interest in both my research and service. As required by union rules and department guidelines, I summarized the meaning of all this in a narrative description and provided hard copies of my evidence. Incredibly when I won my tenure battle at Green University, Baby, who was born near the time that I finished the application, had a lot to do with it. All of my past career armament was virtually useless.[14]

On a lovely spring day four months after I had applied, Professor Somoe, chairperson of the department's personnel committee, called me at home. I was somewhat startled as Somoe's unusually pleasant tones reached through the telephone lines and disturbed my morning ritual of nursing during a day that I was scheduled to be at home. (Schedule flexibility is a traditional advantage of working in higher education.) Professor Somoe explained that the committee wanted to give me an opportunity to present my tenure case to them, but they needed to meet with me within the next two hours. I asked for a delay due to the fact that I was a nursing mother and did not have anyone to care for my infant. Professor Somoe responded, making an unreasonable demand sound routine, "Well, we want to give you the opportunity to speak to your application, but we cannot wait because our decision is due at the university personnel committee tomorrow morning." I reasoned, "My job is at stake because of a formality. Everyone who has applied for tenure at Green University has gotten it." I hurried to locate my copy of the three-pound tenure application, stuffed it into the diaper bag along with Baby's toiletries, installed a car seat, packed Baby into the seat, and set out for the university, located about half an hour from our home.

I dodged in and out of the heavy city traffic and pointed the car toward Green University; concern for safety was lost as I sped to arrive at the appointed time. Slightly out of breath from the rush, I parked and toted Baby across campus with the very

---

[14] Although I may refer to some family members by name, I here I have chosen to use the general term "Baby" and changed many other aspects of this situation so that any similarity to persons living or dead or to the specific timeframe is merely coincidental. My only intent is to help the reader understand the lessons I learned.

heavy diaper bag and weighty tenure application. I panted as I lugged everything into the very small meeting room and sat in a chair before the three-person committee that was chaired by Professor Somoe. Immediately, I could tell that something was not right. No one would look at me; they did not even offer a "hello." Soon it became apparent that this meeting would not be a formality, as Professor Somoe began to read complaints from former students—complaints that I had never heard about before. Apparently, Somoe had been in contact with disgruntled students in my classes while I had been off on maternity leave.

The thrust of Somoe's remarks suggested that I had been irresponsible in dealing with students and that I had provided inadequate proof of the importance of my service and research work. Four of the most damaging charges to my application were (1) I had not told the truth about an instance when I allegedly cancelled a class to attend an uncle's funeral; (2) I had deceived the committee and students because I had not submitted an obituary to prove my funeral attendance (this had never been a part of the departmental procedure before); (3) it was unclear (despite a letter from the producer) that I had actually provided research and service as a consultant on a nationally-distributed documentary about sexual harassment; and (4) even if I had consulted on the documentary, the topic was not necessarily related to social work.

I began to perspire and to feel sick to my stomach—wounded as I made an impromptu attempt to answer the major charges, save my job, and win round one of this tenure game. Just as I began to respond, Baby began to fidget and cry, probably because I had been in such a rush to get to the battleground (meeting) that Baby had not finished the morning nursing. So I covered my breast with a blanket, nursed Baby, and simultaneously began to answer the charges. Several minutes into this gruesome clash with my social work colleagues, Baby had the largest, smelliest bowel movement that one small human could possibly let loose. The outsized odor made by my tiny

145

infant filled the little institutional-yellow cinder block room. I noted that the faces of the committee changed from blank, bored stares to reddened grimaces, and Professor Somoe said, "I think we have heard enough. You are dismissed."

It took a long time to clean up Baby's waste, but it had saved me from dealing with more of the foul activity in that room! Thanks to Baby, I escaped the round bruised but not bowed enough to give up the entire game: the tenure battle. As I retraced my steps with my infant and all my other heavy belongings, I was convinced that I had been dealt with unfairly, capriciously, and outside of the law. The merit of my application had been summarily disregarded. I needed more reinforcements or allies—besides Baby—to win.

As I suspected would happen, the departmental personnel committee recommended to the university personnel committee that my employment should be terminated, that I should not receive tenure. The Department Head (DH)—who up to this point had given me all positive feedback—agreed and cited the evidence that had been brought forth in the personnel hearing. I naively believed that the personnel committee had misrepresented and misconstrued my application, that the department head had been misled and that if I submitted rebuttal information, then all would be well. Using the union contract, I filed procedural appeals that were denied at the department level. Thus, two negative recommendations went to the university personnel committee.

When the children were asleep and the house was quiet, then my husband turned to me on the night after the fateful department personnel committee meeting, folded me into his strong arms, and said, "Those people are crazy. What they have done is blatant discrimination against you as a woman. We are not going to let this stand. Everything they did was outside of their own union rules; they are treating you differently (the game must be played with the same rules for all players) than the White guy who went up for tenure, and probably different from anyone else who has ever gone up. This sounds like the stupid things that I investigate at the federal level" (where he was in a civil rights division). Having had my own experience as a civil rights worker, I judged what he said to be true. The hard part would be to prove it. I also knew from experience that even a person with a legitimate compliant has to persevere to win. I was angry—really, really angry—and probably the genesis of my anger was that it seemed to me that a group of biased people had disturbed me in my primal act of nursing and thereby inserted themselves into my infant's bowel tract.

Early in my life, my parents taught me to fight. They commanded me to protect my seven younger brothers and sisters on the playground, and I did this no matter how much bigger or older the opponent might be or whether they were male or female. I always won. (In our one-room elementary school we had a series of teachers, so all of them were not as careful to prevent fights as the one my mother had earlier convinced to watch over the playground.) I was more afraid of my parents' displeasure than I was of the playground bullies, and opponents learned not to pick on me or my siblings. I saw the situation at Green University in much the same way: Bullies wanted me off the playground and had no regard for me or my infant child.

I had a righteous indignation that burned my veins at a white-hot level; this fired my determination to win tenure. My knight in shining armor and husband, Michael, was joined by a second reinforcement that I will call Hannah the Horrible. This woman attorney had been recommended to me by an older colleague who had been around academia for a long time. Hannah's reputation was that she was formidable in battle; she had never lost a civil rights case in decades of legal wrangling with universities. When I entered her office, I was comforted by her towering size of well over six feet and a weight in excess of two hundred and fifty pounds, deep voice, and firm handshake. Hannah told me that I would likely win the ultimate battle for this job because both the department personnel committee and director had acted arbitrarily and capriciously (with malice) when they had not provided proper notification to me of the hearing, a reasonable opportunity to provide contrary evidence, or given written notice of stated charges. Additionally, all of the procedures and evidence of negative evaluation used by the departmental personnel committee were outside of the union (game) rules for Green University.

Hannah had to be paid in advance. Her services cost my family the equivalent of a week's vacation at Disney World, but I had no regrets about it when I saw the letter (guided missile) that she directed to the provost's office about my case. Most important, during our first consultation, Hannah tipped her very sturdy leather chair back and fixed her deep-set tiny dark eyes on me, and said, "Look, you're going to win this thing—not at the department level because they have a grudge match going, precisely what they are not allowed to do. They're in it to win, but if not, they'll be satisfied to wring every ounce of worry that they can from you. Your task is to file a union grievance now that your procedural appeal has been denied. You already paid the union with your dues; let them do their job. Next you will put your case to the university personnel committee, and then relax about the outcome (battle). You will win at the provost's level; you will get tenure. Just don't plan for a kiss and make up with your department because that ain't never gonna happen. We don't want to go to court, although I certainly could win this case there. What would their defense be of an impromptu hearing with a nursing mother? There is none; they have violated your civil rights as a woman. Once the provost's office of Green University gets my letter, I am sure that they will see the value to grant you tenure."

Just prior to my university hearing, some students came to tell me what had happened during my maternity leave. They also put their statements in writing to the university personnel committee and said, in effect, that Prof. Somoe had organized a

148

public meeting with students to ask if anyone would like to complain about my teaching. The students believed that Prof. Somoe's actions were wrong, and they told me that they had no complaints because they learned a lot from me. Additionally, they volunteered to appear at the hearing where I made the point that Somoe's actions, and that of the committee and department head, were outside of the union procedures, questionable on the legal basis of discrimination against me as a woman, and unethical by social work standards, which require colleagues to discuss differences with each other.

Hannah's prediction came true. The university personnel committee recommended to the provost that I receive tenure. The game was not over, because first the provost had to make his recommendation, and then the regents had to review it to decide if tenure would be granted. As Hannah had requested, I filed the grievance against my department and won. During all of these skirmishes my shining knight, Michael, cheered me on when I was scared and unsure, and he kept me focused on the logic of Hannah's plan when I just wanted to have hand-to-hand combat. He helped me to remember the value of the famous Chicago saying, "Don't get mad. Get even." The provost of the university recommended that I receive tenure, and the Board of Regents concurred with his recommendation.

Another famous statement comes to mind here. I first heard a Mafia don use it in the movie, *The Godfather,* to describe the deaths and mayhem part of the mob's activities: "It's just business." To me, as a person of color and first-generation woman, "just business" means that I have learned, after too many pitfalls and tears, to expect that out of earshot my colleagues may say, "You know she is just not our kind. She doesn't fit in here." Furthermore, based on my experience at Green University and other institutions of higher education, faculty colleagues make harsh judgments about untenured faculty, and plan to take action in secret, often before the formal process begins. Universities can make decisions to hire, terminate, or not grant permanent status to employees based on personalities or rules made up after the fact, as long as they don't have a pattern of such behavior with protected classes (women or minorities). My experience at Green University suggested to me that it is the business of universities to get the best personality or research fit—a popularity contest—at any given time using any means necessary unless caught. Some might call this cheating, or, as the Mafia Don says, "Just business."

After this, one of the university administrators offered me an assignment as director of a new project. Faculty often move into and out of their departments to administrative assignments or special tasks for various levels of government. Their tenure is not affected by these changes. Therefore, I left the tense department behind and took my promotion—which I had applied for concurrent to tenure—and an increase in pay with me to this new assignment. I enjoyed the new work immensely, and coincidentally was assigned to receive further training about how to work most effectively in a "collegial" environment. I am proud to say that my program team had great service outcomes and that in the process I gained greater wisdom and experience. A couple of years into the project, I asked the administrator why she had recruited me for such a great opportunity. Her answer was, "I could see you had tenacity and talent from how you handled yourself with your department."

While on my administrative assignment, I learned from many whispered conversations with others who knew all the players that I had made some early strategic blunders in my department, for which my colleagues there had vowed to take revenge. First and foremost, I had ignored Prof. Somoe's initial advice to me about teaching. "We don't have to work too hard here," Somoe said. "This is not a hard job as long as you don't expect too much from the students; they are not really very capable of much. What I do is, I save myself time and instead of holding classes I have individual conferences for three or four weeks during each semester. This way I can talk to them individually about their work. We do not have a really hard job." Seeking further guidance on this issue, I asked the department head if I should cancel classes for a number of weeks to have individual conferences. The department head told me that we were all expected to hold classes routinely. Unbeknownst to me, when I asked questions about the routine conduct of class I had ignited Prof. Somoe's animosity.

Prof. Enie, the White man who had also sought tenure, explained his vote (yes, the rules allowed him to compete for tenure and to vote on another applicant) to me. "While you were on maternity leave I was very sick, to the point that I could not even get out of bed to call in so students could be notified; this happened several times. The other faculty told me that I would either have to vote against you or be terminated for cause. I am so sorry." Prof. Enie looked directly into my eyes as a few tears formed and spilled onto his cheeks; his being seemed to recede even further into his formerly handsome and robust face, which was now a puffy yellow. He forced words from a down-turned mouth to explain, "Somoe does hate you. You messed up a sweet deal. Somoe used to work about half the time for full-time pay. However, if it is possible, Prof. Mynnie hates you even more and with a passion."

Prof. Enie reminded me of my second offense, which dealt with a very delicate issue. Several students had alleged instances of sexual misconduct to me that involved Prof. Mynnie, an elegant young man. A severely disabled social work student taking a class from Mynnie had been seduced into performing sexual favors for him. Two other students had spoken at length to the student and repeated very specific details of their encounters to me. Incredulous, I went to the department head (DH) about this; the DH suggested that we bring the issue up in faculty meeting. When the time came to raise the issue, I was the sole voice to repeat the allegations. I had figured that the students might have exaggerated the situation and actually expected Prof. Mynnie to deny all charges and to ask for an investigation. He did neither of these things, but glowered at me from that day forward, only speaking when I spoke directly to him. On the positive side of the ledger, the student complaints ceased. Apparently, Prof. Mynnie no longer had a relationship with the disabled student or others, but he had bided his time to take revenge for this infringement on his sex life. My former friend and very ill colleague said in a strangled voice, "He is so glad you got promoted to administration—out of the way whenever he wants to resume his former habits!" Shortly after this conversation, Professor Enie died.

From this and other conversations, I realized that I had learned too late not to discuss sensitive personnel questions with the DH. Members of my profession are supposed to honor confidential discussions between themselves and clients, but also with other social workers in the job setting. I learned the hard way that this DH did not honor the social work ethic of confidentiality when it came to supervising me. As a newcomer to academic life, I also discovered that DH's job security relied upon the votes of the other faculty members, and since they had decided to act in a bloc during my maternity leave, agreement had been reached among them to renew the DH's time in the position, which carried with it some financial rewards. Additionally, I had crusaded for the underdog, the disabled student, but in doing so I had earned a very cunning and determined enemy. These scenarios of "collegial governing" arrangements had been beyond my comprehension, leaving me with no ability to develop an effective strategy to protect myself. In the years since I confronted this situation at Green University, all levels of government prohibit sexual discrimination, and institutions of higher education are much more aggressive as they orient new faculty on appropriate behaviors. There are written procedures to investigate such complaints, and staff allocated to investigate. When President Barack Obama signed the Lily Ledbetter Act during the first months of his first term in office, more investigators became available due to an increase in funding, so that the Office of Equal Employment Opportunity Commission more vigorously enforces the laws that deal with workplace discrimination. However, new hires who seek tenure still take a significant risk if they report or discuss a senior colleague's alleged sexual behavior on the job when it involves current consumers of service (which is always a violation of social work ethics and can lead to loss of a professional license), other colleagues, or subordinates. This is now termed by law as sexual harassment, particularly if it is unwanted and repeated.

I have lost and won during two other tenure processes. The one I lost, I believe, was largely due to the grief that I suffered when, within one year, my father, a dear uncle, and a dear aunt died. Simultaneously, I suffered three potentially life-threatening illnesses that went undiagnosed for a year or more in my first three years at my new university. In short, I could not meet the expectations of the job, given my physical and emotional condition. This was a traumatic time, but a mentor told me about a faculty position at Eastern Michigan University (EMU). So I have won two rounds of the tenure game and lost one. My last win, EMU, became my academic home for over 17 years. I retired from EMU in 2013.

Although I had been seasoned enough by my experience at Green University to gain tenure at EMU once my health stabilized, I have found that one secret to success as a tenure-track faculty is similar to my philosophy of a good love affair: Never give it everything that you've got. Sure, put effort into it, but save enough of yourself so that you can survive if it doesn't work out. Always have an alternative in mind; you must keep your research, serve the public, and teach at a level that another suitor will find you attractive—preferably a more dashing one.

Quoted in a 2010 book review, Dr. Lee Bolinger, President of Columbia University, gave some good advice in regard to failure to gain admission to a college; I believe it relates more generally to failure to gain contract renewal or tenure:

To . . . allow other people's assessment of you to determine your own self-assessment is a very big mistake. The question really is, who at the end of the day is going to make the determination about what your talents are, and what your interests are? That has to be you. (as cited in Shellenbarger, 2010)

Reference

Shellenbarger, S. (2010, March 24). Rejected: Before they were titans, moguls, and newsmakers, these people were... rejected. *Wall Street Journal*, pp. D1, D2.

Lessons

1. The civil rights agencies such as the federal Equal Employment Opportunity Commission (located in every state) are responsible for enforcement of laws related to discrimination; you should know your rights under federal laws. These include the Civil Rights Act of 1964; Lilly Ledbetter Fair Pay Act of 2009; Age Discrimination in Employment Act of 1967; Title IX of the Education Amendments of 1972; Equal Opportunities Act of 1974, and the Americans with Disabilities Act of 1990. You can find information on these and other laws in libraries or go to the federal website, http://www.eeoc.gov.

2. The players and rules for annual review, third year review, and tenure change over time and within colleges and universities. Before you accept a job, I would encourage job candidates to meet with a union representative if the institution is unionized; if it is not, ask for a copy of the

faculty human resource procedures and rules. You should speak to tenured and untenured faculty to ask them to describe the procedure and the role of the potential personnel committee, department head, university personnel committee, provost, and board of governors or regents. Ask what the rate of successful tenure application has been over the last 10 years in your department or school and university-wide. The way they handle your requests may suggest something about the quality and openness of their personnel procedures.

3. I believe that it is wise to keep one's eyes open for new job prospects. You can find out about leads from professional announcements, groups or associations in your discipline, and whenever you attend alumni events. These tactics can help you to build beyond the faculty and to develop a network of other professionals who know you and your work and who can provide you with positive encouragement and information, especially about job opportunities.

4. Come out of the box as fast as possible, but know that the first years as an assistant professor may be rough; it is a hazing process to see if you have what it takes.

5. Develop your personal team. Once you find someone like a husband, parent, friend, co-author, attorney (if necessary) or a more senior colleague who preferably does not work in your department, you will help them to help you if you share rules, procedures, trials, and triumphs. Optimally, your team members need to be patient because they will often need to listen to you when you are most vulnerable to make a mistake, when you are white-hot with anger. You may find it useful to have one of your team members review strategic memos or drafts of articles.

6. Although I learned these lessons during struggles in a university situation, I would recommend that all professional employees consider them.

Chapter 8 —Lessons from the Second Generation

I will reach my goal.
I will because I can.
I can because I know.
I know because I believe.
I believe because my parents told me so.
Personal Mantra – Michael J. Chappell.

We agreed that our children should not be spoiled, meaning that they should work hard for everything they earned so they could ultimately survive without us. We realized that they had financial advantages that we did not have, and we believed that they would be subjected to the lower expectations that almost all African Americans experience. However, we did not have a road map on how best to help our kids. The stories of our children, the second generation to graduate from college, are offered to illustrate some of the hard-won lessons that Michael and I learned.

Aisha – Sittin' Pretty in New York City

"I know where I am.

"I know where all my possessions are—right next to me. There is no need for all this fuss, Mom," stated my calm and reasonable daughter as she enunciated every word as if to reach me more precisely over the several hundred miles which separated us.

I screeched back at her, "*Aisha*! You are on a park bench in New York City!"

"Yes, Mom, but it is beautiful here," she said soothingly. "I'm safe. You remember the park near our hotel? It's beautiful. It's safe," said my daughter. I pictured her glancing around the preternaturally quiet park nestled among tall residential buildings and located near the historic Gramercy Hotel where we had stayed on our recent trip from Detroit for her job interview. She undoubtedly saw the sun-dappled leaves, the broad manicured lawn where toddlers, mommies, and nannies enjoyed the weather, which was reportedly just above eighty degrees. Two nagging thoughts flashed onto the screen of my mind's eye: How did Aisha get into the park unnoticed with all of her gear? If she was there, then couldn't less savory characters enter, too?

My daughter's precious life flashed before my eyes. She was a newborn baby so exquisitely beautiful that hours after her birth, janitors, nurses, and other patients came by to compliment and admire her. In our household of loud, intelligent, argumentative, and sometimes brash people, Aisha was quiet. She was so painfully shy and quiet in kindergarten that when she went to first grade the school administrators placed her in a remedial class; we discovered that she always said she did not know an answer to a question because she didn't want to risk being wrong. This is how she tried to be a quiet good little girl in school. I believe that Aisha's initial lack of progress was in large measure due to my lack of focus on her because I was absorbed in my own education as a doctoral student. Her remedial placement served as a wake-up call for all of us.

Michael and I had the wonderful assistance of Aisha's second-grade teacher, Shirley Reid, as we helped Aisha to develop confidence, academic skills, and assertiveness. We helped Aisha to read the books that Mrs. Reid supplied. We read more books to her at night. We nominated her for most improved student in her grade. Mrs. Reid cast Aisha as the Mother Kitten in a play. Within a year Aisha's grades improved from remedial level to *B* in the mainstream class, then the next year *A-*, and from there it was watch out! Aisha developed into a fine student and became an athlete.

As an athlete she competed with adults in three-mile races at nine years of age. ("Dad, do we have to wait for Mom? No, then let's go!" she said as her long braids flew by me.) I recalled the glorious bloom of young womanhood as her lithe legs carried her over hurdles during high school track competitions; the Big-Ten Conference later named her a scholar-athlete for her record at University of Michigan.

Even with her athletic and academic achievements, which I admire greatly, as an adult our daughter is generally a quiet and tactful person, perhaps honed by the Christian debutante training that she got at Hartford Baptist Church. Aisha has never met an enemy in her life. Since early childhood she has had an unearthly ability to focus her cheerful and beautiful being almost completely on whomever she is speaking to. You feel as though the sun is on your face when you look into her big brown eyes and feel that she is interested—to the exclusion of all else—in what you have to say, your life, and concerns.

Aisha had just graduated from Michigan with dual degrees in Economics and Spanish only two weeks prior to "taking up residence" on her park bench.

I turned and looked at my phone longingly, and I began to reflect upon how much I loved this small package of dynamite – 5'8" and 130 pounds of muscle, bone, and determination (who my mother called "A little piece of leather but well put together"). Along with her physical maturity, Aisha's personality morphed from that of a shy and insightful child to that of a self-assured young woman. As a very young child she would let her friends or her brother boss her around until I interceded and pointed out that she needed to know what she wanted and tell others, even argue her point if necessary. This proved very difficult for Aisha, who had legions of friends in part because she was undemanding and attentive, but as she reached puberty my daughter grew exponentially in assertiveness. During middle school and into high school she became equally adept at listening and telling her friends what she thought, to the extent that she was elected an officer of the Honors Society. The coaches also selected her as co-captain of both her high school track and cross-country teams.

As everyone around me clapped in joy, I cried when the coach announced Aisha's second captain's position. I had counted on stretching to fulfill the parental expectations to organize meals, attend all meets, and collect money for the Cross Team (over 70 girls). I also knew that the parents' workload would be a difficult challenge for me because I had a full-time job and experienced fainting spells associated with rather extraordinary pain from "female problems." When Michael saw my tears, he assured me that he would take parental leadership for the track team. He kept his word and both teams, track and women's cross country, went on to great seasons as we usually tagged along dragging tents, food, and water.

To be honest, thinking about all our parental effort, I believed that my daughter owed me a greater measure of caution now that she was in New York City. My mind equated this situation to a slot machine that has been stuffed with coins and should be ready to pay out. My husband and I had given Aisha all the time (see above) and attention (coins into the slot) we were capable of giving to her physical, social, academic, and cultural development: enumerable teachers' conferences, attendance at blaringly bad music rehearsals, midnight edits of her papers, excellent medical and dental care, sponsorship for her to become a Christian debutante, and tedious arguments about dress and conduct. Then to top it all off we put up with really, really, seriously bad teenage attitude. She had the kind of bad attitude that suggests adoption even in the later teen years. Her attitude at least 6 days a week (she slept or talked to her friends on the seventh day) was a sneer and mumble about our aged stupidity or impossibly bad taste in clothing, cars, hair style, make-up, food choice, or anything else she could think about. So the payout that we were looking for from our daughter/slot machine was: *stay alive*! Don't take unnecessary risks by residing on a park bench with all your stuff in New York City.

My reverie was interrupted. "M-O-T-H-E-R! I am twenty-two. Calm down. Now, it is true," she patiently explained to me, "that I do not currently have a place to stay. However, I am sure that my friend, Maya, will call me soon and tell me where to hook up for the night. You know I do have a job, and I have many college friends in this city."

Swallowing to keep the razor's edge of fear out of my voice, I suggested, "Aisha, glance around the park. Do you see any 'seedy' characters watching you?"

"No, Mother." She answered in her dismissively calm tone. My daughter has never had a sense of danger. Undoubtedly, this is partly because she was raised in a quiet suburb and because she judged herself, as an elite athlete who had competed for state honors, to be faster and stronger than most people.

"Okay," I said as I let my breath out slowly. Then I panicked again thinking about the potential danger of millions upon millions of criminal types who might descend on my child. I screeched rapid-fire questions over the 600-plus miles that separated us. "What time does that park close? What are your alternate plans for the night? What time do you go to work tomorrow? Why didn't Maya call you earlier?"

"Mom, it will be okay," she said.

I said with determination, "Listen, Aisha, if you don't find your friend by 5 p.m. when it starts to get dark, then please promise me that you will check into the Gramercy Hotel. *Please* use the credit card that I gave you," I said, begging for her safety and coincidentally more debt.

"Yes, Mom." We were interrupted by a series of clicks on the line, and I guessed that this was a signal for an incoming call— maybe the friend, Maya, with a safe haven for my baby girl? "I got to go," she said.

"Bye." I pleaded. "Call me if it isn't her?"

"Okay," Aisha said hurriedly.

New York City did work out well—in a way. Aisha stayed with Maya. For a week she went to work, got trained to be a teacher, and began to earn money. Then both Maya and Aisha were evicted! It turned out that Maya had a verbal lease agreement, and the landlady was quite unhappy to realize that the bushy-haired "White" tenant she had rented to was in fact a fair-complexioned African-American woman who had an obviously African-American friend, Aisha. You know, "birds of a feather flock together." The girls took this rejection in stride: They called the landlady a crazy racist who was not worthy of additional discussion. Subsequently, the two African-American "homeless" girls frantically searched for lodging and landed an apartment in the borough of Queens—a two-hour work commute each day for Aisha, but it was affordable on a teacher's modest starting salary.

There were other episodes of things not quite working out: The apartment ceiling fell on Aisha (missing vital organs because of her quick reflexes but leaving a small scar on her forehead), the landlord refused to reimburse her for the damages until legal action commenced, the burn she suffered from an exposed pipe in the bathroom, and the mugger scared off when Maya used her five-octave singing voice to let loose a string of obscenities as the two young women blithely strolled home from bar-hopping at 5 a.m.

These adventures further solidified my aversion to New York City. Luckily, my daughter has stayed safe through the last several years as she has become a seasoned resident. I now realize that my own parents were as terrified for me when I moved into an apartment in the heart of Detroit almost forty years ago, but I also know that there are major differences between their involvement and mine. One, my husband and I had enough finances (mostly credit) to make loans to Aisha for apartment deposits and airline tickets to her new city. Two, we helped her get settled into the city because I planned and accompanied her on the first job-search visit (I had basic knowledge of the city because of prior business trips). Three, we were able to use our "spare time" to purchase or move most of her furniture from Michigan to New York City. Last, as working professionals we could provide advice and counsel on the many pitfalls she faced during that first year on the job, *and* we visited her new home several times a year to provide moral reassurance and support. Her student-teaching supervisor even welcomed us as we visited her classroom; the kids loved meeting us as they noisily asked to hear tales about Aisha at their age. They seemed motivated by her elementary class climb out of remedial classes to become an honors student and later Big-Ten Scholar Athlete.

After the park bench and the damaged couch, Aisha held off for years before buying a permanent place to sit. However, the couch she purchased was a quite elegant green the color of early spring trees; it was well-crafted, strong. The model name is "Betty." One might say that with five years experience as a mathematics teacher in middle school, tenure, promotion, a newly-minted Master's of Education, and now a job as an administrator, that Aisha did all right for herself in the "Big Apple." Actually, one might say that she is sittin' pretty in New York City.

PhD: The Second Generation & M. Jahi Chappell

Once I overheard my son and daughter talking. "You know there are some things that we can't do?" Jahi said to his sister as she nodded assent. "Yes, you know, like if a computer program has a bug in it; we are not going to be able to fix it by force of reason and will."

Aisha, legs and arms sprawled akimbo on the couch, laughed. "Yeah, I have learned that, but I used to waste time trying. Mom and Dad taught us to solve problems. I am always amazed when all problems and situations don't bend to my will."

Jahi, who by this time had written and rewritten one chapter of his dissertation for over a year, continued: "I know that I can finish this PhD. I don't have the exact date, but there is no question in my mind that it can be done." As I overhear this chatter, I think that to me he has done the almost-impossible already. That is, he learned Portuguese in a year and used it to do his research while he lived in Brazil to collect the data he busily analyzed while he talked to his sister. He had even been undaunted when he was robbed during his first weeks in the country while he escorted a young lady on a late-night beach stroll. I had asked Jahi, "Why didn't you use your martial arts skills to prevent the theft?" He told me quite rationally, "Mother, I had so little money that it was not even worth the risk, and there were two robbers."

Resuming their conversation, Aisha added to her brother's analysis of how we had parented them: "For me, it is not can I finish a doctoral degree, but rather do I want to do it and if so, for what reason? In that way we are really lucky people."

Jahi agreed with his sister.

I listened to these two young gifted and Black people—the lights of my life—and wished that the undergraduate students I teach at Eastern Michigan University had the same self-confidence. Psychologists argue that nurture interacts with nature to foster a self-image, a personality, a sense of where one fits in the world, and an assessment of one's intellectual and physical skills. Well, Jahi's nature required a "special" brand of nurturing. My husband and I initially thought that Jahi was possessed, and we later found that he was. He was possessed of an intellect that our school system deemed "gifted." However, before this label was attached to him, as a young child he ran pall-mall from room to room in our house while he talked excitedly to his pretend dog that he nagged me to feed; perhaps these behaviors were one sign that he was special—gifted? In defense of my own sanity, as the stay-at-home parent, I tried mightily to focus his frantic energy into reading books, coloring, painting, going to the park, writing, and playing with friends because otherwise he got the best of me and would amuse himself with activities like banging his head into walls or sleeping very little, day or night.

Jahi gave me a wonderful gift, nature appreciation, after I focused his energy into constructive activities. One time we were in our small backyard and Jahi, about 4 years old, looked up and began running. I asked him, "What are you doing?" He replied, "See that," as he pointed to a ray of sunlight, "I want to catch it." For the first time in my life, I looked at a ray of sunlight, and it was beautiful—even if Jahi did not catch it. Then at eight years old, he cried inconsolably when he found out that the very expensive red roses his father bought for me as a Valentine's Day gift would soon die; he only stopped crying when we coaxed him to take a picture of the flowers—which we still have—so that they would live on forever. Jahi loved all things animal, and that is why we had a turtle, gerbils, and a dog. He learned how to care for our dog, Gremlin, so well that she lived to be seventeen years old; we all grew to love that feisty, shaggy, cheerful little dog. He also wrote poetry about nature and was my willing partner in monthly visits to Brookfield Zoo, an internationally renowned park within fifteen minutes of our home. (I had idolized this zoo since childhood when I watched a television show broadcast from that location. Once my parents took us to Brookfield, but the effort to get nine family members from Michigan to Illinois meant that we arrived one hour before closing time.) We even visited during winter snowstorms as both an amusement and because I knew we would be almost alone with the primates in a warm tropical setting. Jahi asked me to become a member of the World Wild Life Federation so that we could read their monthly magazine and talk about the articles; he encouraged the entire family to watch shows about the environment. Thus, all four of us ultimately gained a much better understanding about our natural world because of Jahi.

As he moved from childhood to young adulthood, Jahi shifted his frantic need for external activities to voracious reading and memorizing *witty* material like encyclopedias about nature, although he wasn't quite as good at memorizing jokes for our annual Chappell New Year's Eve talent show because he would laugh before he got to the punch line. As a junior high student he had an organic garden and then founded an ecology club; when he graduated from high school he was chosen as one of the top 20 admits to the University of Michigan based on a 99 percentile standardized test score, a fleet of school activities, and an *A+* grade point average (student's mathematical cumulative record of courses), which he gained when he took advanced placement courses. Later when his dissertation chairperson asked him how he came to understand and love nature, Jahi replied, "My mom took us to the zoo a lot."

Jahi's interest in nature extended to an early curiosity about sex. When I was pregnant with Aisha and he was two and a half years old I got him a book, *Where Did I Come From,* by Peter Mayle (1973). This book explained procreation and sex to very young children, and Jahi thought, rationally, that all the other children in his daycare group should know the same information, but the teacher took me aside and let me know in whispered tones, "Mrs. Chappell, *I* approve of the book, but I think we should let the other parents decide when to provide sex education to their children." I had to explain this to Jahi, who went along but figured that the other children were missing out on some important information. Jahi's natural questions after he read the book were: "Well, Mom, who am I going to marry? What is her name and where does she live?" My husband told me not to encourage him to think along those lines as the other parents would not understand his interest at this early stage of life.

In his quest for sexual understanding, Jahi continued his review of his favorite book during a family trip. As we exited the interstate highway and approached my parents' Michigan home after the three-hour ride from Illinois, he said, "Grandpa has a penis?" We replied, "Yes, that's correct, he does have one," and we hoped that would be enough of an answer. Then he repeated the same question for each of his uncles. Finally, as we pulled into my parents' driveway he said, "But Grandma—she has no penis." We agreed with this assessment and prayed that he would not take his inquiries into my parents' home because they were extremely modest for people who had eight children. Luckily, having exhausted his inquiry, Jahi closed his favorite book and left the penis topic alone during our visit.

Jahi is a feminist. He thinks it is the logical way to see the world. By this I mean that for the most part, he does not believe in the social conventions of sex roles; he has consistently acted on this belief since the age of four. When I took Jahi to his first day of kindergarten, he wanted to take his Black rag doll whose name was also Jahi. I explained that other kids might laugh at him as he pushed the doll's carriage to the school. He turned to me and drew himself up to full height and said, "Mommy, that will be their problem." He marched right up to the school entrance as he pushed his doll in its carriage; then he looked back at me and told me that I could take Jahi doll back home. Instead of traditional sex roles, as a man, Jahi believes that women can and should ask him out on dates, and he will do the same. He believes in sharing expenses. He gives the women that he cares about gifts that will touch their hearts, such as a home-cooked gourmet meal, organic chocolates, fair-trade coffee, and art or photographs of good times, and he is appreciative of similar gifts. He really does not like to flirt or to be involved with romantic drama. He prefers self-assured women with an adventurous spirit who can laugh and exhibit honest emotion and who have a good sense of humor. He seeks a life partner who is his intellectual and economic equal. As aging parents in need of grandchildren, my husband and I are always on the lookout for good candidates, but we have learned that we must let Jahi determine who is a sufficient feminist among his love-interests.

"Mrs. Chappell," said the prim young woman who was my son's teacher, "You should be quite proud of Jahi because he will likely obtain all *C*'s this first marking period of second grade." Knowing that Jahi had earned the highest possible scores on his most recent standardized examination, I replied, "Well, have you reviewed his test scores? Because that is significantly below his potential." The teacher admitted that she had not done so. I pressed on, "Well as a college professor myself, I want to ask you what your pedagogical (teaching) methods are because I would expect his grades to match the potential of his exceptional scores and be in the *A* range." The teacher became flustered at this line of questions but suggested that perhaps Jahi should be in the gifted program. She immediately recommended him to the program, and he thrived from that point on. When my husband and I discussed this incident, we concluded that because Jahi was a Black male child, his potential had been underestimated (there were virtually no Black males on the honor roll). We vowed to monitor his progress, and later his sister's, more closely as we reviewed homework nightly and attended every parent-teacher meeting and school activity that we could. Michael was even elected to be an officer of the PTA. We always asked, no matter what grades they got, "How can our child do better?" We believe that everyone has room for improvement and that the job of parents and teachers is to help the student develop to their maximum capacity.

When Michael and I asked our children to name our greatest contribution to their success as adults, their answers surprised us. Jahi said, "When I tried to get away with things such as not completing my homework before going to a party, sometimes I could get by one of you. But there was always the second person that caught me." Aisha responded, "Once I really didn't want to be an *A* student anymore, but you all weren't having any of it!" She referred to a very trying time in our lives when my mother-in-law became quite ill and simultaneously Aisha decided that she would stop turning in all her homework or studying for tests in a timely fashion; we used what little energy we had left over from work and my mother-in-law's illness to monitor a contract for homework with Aisha. We monitored both of our children's academic progress quite closely, but it took Aisha a little longer to realize that we would watch through both hard times and successes.

Not long after my children's conversation about self-confidence, I learned that my university had received a grant for the McNair Scholars Program, which is named for Dr. Ronald McNair, the MIT-trained African-American astronaut who perished in the Challenger Space crash in 1986. I applied for this position and was selected to direct the program that is targeted at low-income and first-generation students who exhibit academic talent. In essence, this program's goals are not only to provide research skills but also to foster students' self-confidence so that they can successfully complete college and then a doctoral degree in their chosen profession. Thus, in very short order, I got my wish to help university students gain self-confidence in their abilities.

I had an opportunity to assist McNair Scholars and unexpectedly to help Jahi to become a second-generation doctor of philosophy. In January of 2008 I walked into my new corner office in the dilapidated but historic Starkweather Hall where there was a great deal of dust and broken furniture but not much else. Within the next month I hired staff, set up procedures, admitted students, convened a student selection committee, and began a recruitment program so that we could achieve the stated goals in our federal grant. Six months later Jahi's dissertation chairperson, Dr. John Vandermeer, the Asa Gray Distinguished Professor of Ecology and Evolutionary Biology at nearby University of Michigan, required him to complete the last phase of his dissertation with daily writing submissions. During this time Jahi returned home from his campus apartment to live with my husband and me. This move was actually lucky for me. It reminded me of the total devotion necessary to complete a dissertation because while Jahi wrote, my husband and I took care of all his personal needs. We shopped, cleaned, ironed, ran errands, and cooked for him, while we also provided continuous pep talks and did the occasional editorial chore. Jahi did his part as he bathed infrequently, kindly allowed me to tend to his cat (I am *very* allergic to cats), and slept for only a few hours each night. The result of this marathon was that a petite (5' 2" in heels) President Mary Sue Coleman handed a tall (6'1"), handsome young man (called "Brown Sugar" by his Grandma Brown), Michael Jahi Chappell, his doctoral degree from the University of Michigan on a beautiful sunlit day in May 2009.

I lived through this physically and mentally taxing experience with my son while Steven (a pseudonym), a McNair Scholar at Eastern, also approached graduation day with a fear of failure. After a conference with the student's faculty advisor, the three of us determined that Steven would also submit daily evidence of written progress on his final project; we borrowed Dr. Vandermeer's approach to Jahi. I recognized that Steven had some of the same quest for perfection known as "writer's block" that my son had. Additionally, I saw a similar level of loneliness in both men to that I had experienced when confronted by the extraordinary task of writing my own dissertation. Thus, Steven's advisor and I both offered to support him by daily and sometimes twice daily email contacts. Some midnights when I was restless, I would log onto my computer to send a note of cheer to Steven. I might say, "Do not let your fear of success overwhelm your remarkable potential." He might respond, "Thank you, I will put on coffee and get back to writing." Steven got an excellent grade on his project, and when he walked across the university stage to receive his degree, I was there to congratulate him.

Reference

Mayle, P. (1973). *Where did I come from?* Secaucus, NJ: Lyle Stuart.

Lessons from the Second Generation

1. To complete a degree you need support. Friends and family regardless of your financial situation will be important, but be grateful to whoever provides you with support.

2. Mentors can make or break the student who seeks a degree; choose wisely someone who has a reputation as "student-centered." That is, someone who is sympathetic to students' situation, demands the best, but who can also facilitate achievement (reading extra drafts, sending scholarship information, or fitting you into a tight schedule).

3. Self-discipline is more than studying a lot or being very smart; it is also allowing "good enough" to be sufficient. Let others, such as a faculty mentor, guide you to what is "good enough."

4. Parents of K-12 students must monitor and advocate for their children regardless of any natural talents that they may have, but we must often put in the time or find the resources (such as a tutor) to help them excel.

5. Do not give problems such as underachievement, racism, improper classroom placement, or failure to complete homework a chance to grow into larger problems. You should take a look at homework nightly, talk to high school-age children about their struggles, listen to successes, and attend conferences with teachers early and often. Parents are the best advocates a K-12 child can have.

6. We will always need other people who have our best interests at heart. Despite social expectations to be independent, the adult child may need financial and moral support to succeed. We have found that visits and conversations about all aspects of their lives help us to be senior friends to our children. We try to keep them updated on our lives too.

7. Children are individuals who should be engaged in large measure based upon their interests and talents. When you can foster individuality rather than competition, then members of a family can grow together and thus decrease sibling jealousy. We were surprised to find out how much our children could give to us.

Study Questions for Students

1. What start-up costs do you estimate after college? How do expect to get this money?
2. Who can you count on when times are down? What role do you want your parents to play in your adult life? What will you need to do to make this happen?

Chapter 9 — *Blueberry Blessings: Conclusion*

> You know that blueberries are good for you. But did you know that blueberries could help fight aging, combat disease, blood pressure, protect the heart and brain and even boost your memory? (Galland, 2011, para. 1)

This article, similar to many that I have read over the past fifty-plus years, argues something that my family knew long ago—blueberries are good for you. We ate them in pancakes, waffles, pies, muffins, cereal, and straight off the bushes in the field. In an example of historical irony, our father named his business Brown and Sons Blueberry Plantation—a name that has always made my husband cringe. Plantations recall the bad old days when African Americans were labeled by the United States Constitution to be legally three-fifths of a man, beasts. Yet this business that had an odd name contributed mightily to my family's move out of poverty.

As I recall, shortly after my parents paid off their first mortgage and purchased land to build a larger house for their rapidly growing family, they also settled on the idea to attempt to cultivate blueberry bushes. I would place the date between 1955 and 1960 because that is when my mother got a small inheritance that provided a down payment on land to build the new house. Having tried many different crops to earn extra income, Dad and many of our African-American neighbors whose primary income came from their labor at the aluminum foundry noticed that the most prosperous of the surrounding White farmers grew blueberries. They all began to explore what they needed to do to be like this prosperous farmer. Eventually Dad found out that the acidity of soil at both of his holdings would support blueberries; the bushes would take up to four years to reach early maturity. At that time, they could be relied upon to supplement the family's income. He planted and cultivated bushes on both farms, and thus he increased the value of the land, and by the mid-1960s they were indeed yielding a crop that brought in approximately $6000 extra per year. According to my brother, Ben, the highest crop yield was about $24,000, a very tidy profit since Dad's income from the foundry was about $10,000. These bushes helped supplement the family's income from the time I went to college in 1965 until my mother sold the farm in 2005 to underwrite the cost of care for her final illness. At that point, the value of the plantation was at least 10 times its purchase price.

Another reason that farm life—and specifically blueberries—became such a blessing to our family is that we all had to cooperate to cultivate and harvest them. We learned to work as a team, and we learned to endure heat, dirt, bugs, and very long hours to earn the money for our clothing, books, and entertainment. Many of my siblings and I still marvel at how hard we worked, but it is that work ethic that allowed us to all earn college degrees, to work longer hours and weekends when most others had left for home, and now to use electronic devices to maintain our work commitments as we travel to foreign destinations on assignment.

This work ethic is what I brought to academic life, and it served me well particularly when I was healthy. Of course, it is somewhat of a double-edged sword, because I was initially unaware that others, such as Prof. Somoe at Green University, do not have the same ethic. When I challenge students to achieve at their highest possible capability, they sometimes grumble. However, most of the students I teach at Eastern Michigan University have the same dilemma that I faced: high aspirations with low income. At this juncture, I have observed few if any first-generation, low-income, or underrepresented individuals who have been able to achieve great things without herculean effort.

Yet my country upbringing, fierce determination to succeed, joy in education, and anger at injustice have given me a fine life. Despite the bumps in the road, I have found the academic life to be a great reward; it allowed a flexible schedule and thus facilitated my roles as wife and mother, plus I had a lot to say about my course assignments, and I could choose the focus of my research and service. I have had the benefit of all of these positives while getting paid enough that I could provide for my family.

Although I have discussed a number of obstacles in my career as a means to help others avoid or prepare for them, I believe that overall my life has been blessed. At a recent faculty meeting, Professor Elvia Krajewski-Jaime said, "It is all worth it—no matter how hard we work—when you see the students cross the stage, and they thank you. Their faces are so happy, and they have such promise." As a policy professor, I am also warmed by the knowledge that so many of my former students have prospered in my area of teaching: as an aide in the federal Department of Health and Human Services, as an analyst for the National Association of Social Workers, as directors of programs and agencies, as an associate principal of a very large school system, as a state director for the Obama campaign, and as a policy professor in a school of social work.

In 2012, my family awarded the first two Brown-Chappell Scholarships from a fund that my husband and I established at Eastern. I learned enough about team work and giving back from my family that we are so proud and blessed to give to others like ourselves a blueberry blessing that I never could have imagined when I was a child. It is my hope that my two children, Jahi and Aisha, will also be involved with this scholarship for the foreseeable future as they too have been blessed through the generations. They also like blueberries, and we have two bushes from the Brown and Sons Plantation in my backyard. There should be plenty of blueberries for future generations.

Reference

Galland, L. (2011, June 15). Surprising benefits of blueberries. *Huffington Post Live - Healthy Living.* Retrieved from http://www.huffingtonpost.com

Appendix
A Short Discussion of Our Roles as Parents Before, During, and After College
With Michael J. Chappell

1. Nature/nuture. You can start where your child is when you enhance their temperament (nature) or personality with interest in things they find interesting (nuture). When you recognize their individuality you let them lead the way to as many different experiences as possible. Then let them choose according to availability, your financial resources, or those experiences and activities that you can identify for free or where a scholarship may be available.

2. A friend once told us, "God protects us because he does not give us two children exactly alike." Our friend was absolutely correct. This, however, is a blessing and a curse. Your nurturing must be adjusted to each child's nature. Whenever possible, let their nature lead you.

3. Consistency begets self-discipline. By this we mean when you ALWAYS expect the same thing in the same situations. For example, Aisha should do her homework on time and turn it in with very rare exceptions, or Jahi should always do homework before going to a party. Consistency in parents' behavior fosters self-discipline in the child.

4. How does one behave consistently? You should state what is expected, monitor (actually see the printed outcome or hear the speech) to see if it is achieved, provide support such as a tutor or counselor when you find that your skills in an area are not sufficient. We had a calendar for almost all of our family tasks, and it included time for research and first tries (drafts) of papers. We gave praise for completion, and we preferred to let the children choose the treat whenever

possible. For smaller achievements we found that verbal praise was enough; larger rewards might be a sleepover, a visit to a park (free), dinner at a restaurant of their choice, or a toy.

5. Expect the best of the child and expect the best for the child so they can live up to whatever their potential might be. Not only did we praise our children for academic or extracurricular achievement, but we also encouraged others—grandparents, teachers and school officials—to provide similar recognition.

6. As our children became adults, we have found it very helpful to view them as the decision-makers about their own lives. The closer they come to the age of majority, the less "hovering" or constant watching one needs to do. As they mature we have taken on the role less of decision-makers and more of "senior" advisors and cheerleaders. It is difficult to know when and how to step back. Let adult children make decisions and help them examine or talk about the consequences. They tend to learn a lot more from decisions they make that don't work than decisions we make or might try to insist upon. Once our children realized we would not try to force our judgment on them, they began to seek our advice. Sometimes they follow it, and sometimes they don't.

7. Your children will not "naturally" know how to love you as an adult child. We have all grown together and tried to learn how best to interface with each others' friends, time schedule, work flow, and hobbies. We have learned to give and receive gifts that all will enjoy.

8. You will love your children differently because they are different people with different needs. A student recently asked Betty which child she cared for more. Here is her

answer: "I love both of my arms, but I do not love one more than the other. I have different abilities with each one, but I do not want to clothe one less than the other or feed one less than the other. I do not take one arm to a favorite restaurant and leave the other home. So it is with my children."